Your Yucatán Guide

Your Yucatán Guide

HENRY F. GODFREY

FUNK & WAGNALLS

First Printing
Copyright © 1967 by Henry F. Godfrey
All rights reserved.
Library of Congress Catalog Card Number: 67–28161
Published by Funk & Wagnalls, *A Division of* Reader's Digest Books, Inc.

Printed in the United States of America

Acknowledgments

Two people have contributed greatly to the interest and usefulness of this book, and I am greatly appreciative.

The cover glyph, and those on the endpapers, are the work of my friend Elsie Freund. These lovely drawings were made by her in the courtyard of the Palace at Palenque, that Maya wonder-city in the jungle-covered mountains of Chiapas. The magnificent jaguar contemplating a human heart is also hers and was sketched at the Platform of the Tigers and Eagles at Chichén Itzá. All have been much praised by both artists and archaeologists, and my thanks go to her for her kind permission to reproduce them here.

The maps or, as the artist Don Bohren persists in calling them, "pictorial signs," are a remarkable combination of imagination and accuracy. They not only perform the primary function of a map as a guide to an area, but by the devices that he has portrayed convey the true feeling of each Maya city as well. Don, too, produced the fascinating drawing of the Ring of the Ball Court at Chichén Itzá, as well as that of one of the arches that break the wall of the old city of Mérida.

My thanks also go to the Instituto Nacional de Antropologia e Historia for permission to reproduce their photograph of the slab from the Funerary Crypt of the Temple of the Inscriptions at Palenque.

HENRY F. GODFREY
DeLand, Florida
July 1967

TO John Lloyd Stephens

I trust that what I have done will give the reader some definite idea of the ruins. Perhaps, as I did, he will imagine the scene that must have been presented when these buildings were entire, occupied by people in costumes strange and fanciful as the ornaments on their buildings, and possessing all those minor arts which must have been coexistent with architecture and sculpture, and which the imperishable stone has survived.

—JOHN LLOYD STEPHENS
Incidents of Travel in Yucatán (1841)

AND TO MY "Pyramid-climbing" Wife whose growing enthusiasm over the beauty and wonder of Yucatán contribute so largely to our mutual enjoyment of the mystery of the ancient Maya.

Contents

List of Illustrations

A section of photographs follows page 85.

Introducing
Yucatán

The Purpose
of This Guide

The sole purpose of this guide is to be useful to you. To be useful in deciding whether—and why—you should go to Yucatán in the first place; what you should see—and why you should see it; how long you should stay in Yucatán—and where you should spend your time; and how best you may enjoy the attractions and facilities that this diverse land offers.

In short, this book is written to enable you to gain the most in pleasure and interest from the Yucatán Peninsula: from its thousand-year-old Maya ruins to its centuries-old Spanish cities to its modern-as-tomorrow vacation spots.

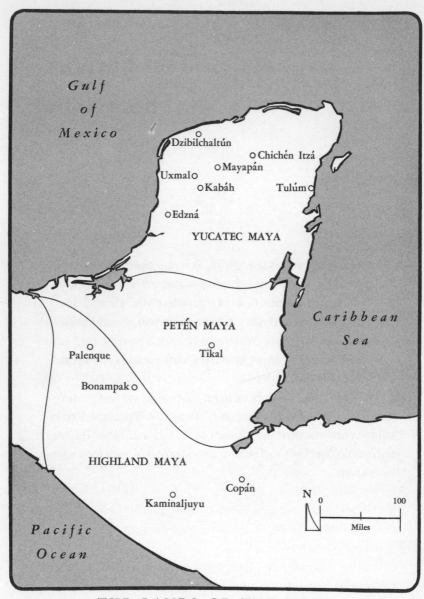

THE LANDS OF THE MAYA

The Land and
Its People

The Yucatán Peninsula projects like a thumb from Central America, northward toward the pointing finger of Florida. It is a flat land, averaging barely twenty feet above sea level. Primarily a limestone plain, it bears only a few skimpy inches of topsoil; it has few rivers, but an illimitable amount of subsurface water. It includes, besides the state of Yucatán, the state of Campeche and the territory of Quintana Roo.

The peninsula is bounded on the south by a low range of hills, stretching from east to west, from Chetumal on the Caribbean to the Laguna de Términos on the Gulf of Mexico.

The ancient Maya, of course, knew no such boundaries. Their land spread south to the Pacific Ocean, expanding somewhat as the peninsula widened at its base, to include Guatemala as well.

Within this area, which today we consider almost impassable jungle, the ancient Maya traveled at will. As a result of this ease of communication, you will notice a distinct similarity of architecture and of religious expression wherever you travel in the "Land of the Maya." While each Maya "city" possesses its own distinctiveness, you will see details that form an underlying pattern— details that you will be delighted to recognize and remember. All travelers feel this happy sense of recollection. One hundred and twenty-five years ago, the great explorer John Lloyd Stephens was writing in his narrative descriptions, "as we saw at" Palenque or Uxmal or Chichén or any of the other dozens of Maya cities that he visited.

You will feel, too, as he did, the lack of any concrete historical background. But you must be resigned to this, for even today there is no real agreement. A book by Charles Gallenkamp is titled: *Maya—The Riddle and Rediscovery of a Lost Civilization,* not "Riddle and Solution."

Even generalities may well be incorrect; or become so as the light of new discoveries reveals facts hitherto unknown. It has, for example, long been a subject of general agreement that the origin of Maya civilization lay in the Guatemala jungle, at Tikal, Uaxactún, or Copán. Yet recent investigation indicates that Dzibilchaltún in northern Yucatán was a city two thousand years before the birth of Christ—and continued as an entity until the Spanish Conquest.

Riddles abound. No Rosetta Stone exists to solve the tremendous volume of glyphs sculptured on imperishable stone. True, it is believed that dates can be interpreted; yet scholars disagree even here, and testing with Carbon 14 provides no conclusive answer. All Maya books were burned as works of the devil by Bishop Landa; and such translations as remain are but the Yucatecans' concept of their history. As S. G. Morley says, "There is evidence in them [the translated books] of considerable garbling through the misplacement of the order of events in time, and a frequent telescoping of the time scale to make successive events contemporaneous."

The greatest puzzle of all is, of course, what made the Maya abandon their great stone cities. For that is exactly what they did. Cities built to last a thousand years or more—as they have done, for you will see them—were deserted almost overnight. They were not destroyed but simply emptied of people, thousands and thousands of people. Why? No one knows. And no theory yields a completely satisfactory answer.

At first the abandonment appears to have been a movement, a long trek. The cities of the Petén, the lowland Guatemalan jungle, were evacuated by their entire populations. Other cities appeared or grew in stature. Palenque, high in the rain forest of Chiapas, near the Gulf of Mexico, was already a major site. Uxmal developed from nothing to become the most beautiful city of the Puuc, the rolling hill country to the southwest of the peninsula. Chichén Itzá had been occupied for two hundred years before it was first abandoned. Why?

Then Palenque disappeared, not to be visited again for seven centuries. Was it conquered by invaders from the mainland? But its delicate, easily destroyed stucco work—of incomparable beauty—remains intact to this day. Why?

Uxmal was snuffed out in an instant. It was founded about A.D. 1000 by the Xiu. Today you may view the Xiu family tree, demonstrating direct descent from the founder of Uxmal. You may even meet the present head of the clan. But no tradition or legend tells you the answer. Why?

Chichén, once abandoned, flourished once again. And once again died. Rumor says that civil war was fought among the cities of Uxmal, Mayapán, and Chichén Itzá. Yet evidence can be presented to show that these cities did not exist concurrently. The city-state of Mayapán did collapse, however, and after its fall all the larger cities were abandoned. Why?

There is no answer. The Maya grew, developing one of the great civilizations of the world, bringing art and architecture to a high degree of excellence—and suddenly ended, leaving behind only the imperishable stone . . . and a pleasant, happy, subservient people.

One of the great achievements of the ancient Maya was their development of an extraordinarily accurate calendar. Only by seeing the figures to the right of the decimal point can you appreciate it: the Gregorian calendar, which we live under today, considers the solar year to consist of 365.2425 days. This figure allows for one Leap Year in every four years, except for a century year, which is only counted as a Leap Year if divisible by four hundred. Science tells us that the actual length of the year is 365.2422 days. The ancient Maya calculated the year as 365.2420 days. And this accuracy was accomplished—perhaps as early as three centuries before Christ—by a people who never in their entire history knew the wheel, or used metal, or possessed a beast of burden.

It is interesting to consider the fact that Bishop Landa, who, for all his destructiveness, knew more about the ancient Maya than any other man, returned to the European continent twenty years before the adoption of the Gregorian calendar. Perhaps it is to the Maya that we owe its useful accuracy.

It may well be that what happened to that tremendous storehouse of intelligence that was the Maya priesthood and upper class provides the key to the abandonment of the Maya cities.

To determine this, you must look more closely at the daily round of the life of the Maya peasant; for he exists today, living very much as did his ancestors a thousand years ago. There is no Maya ruling class today. The Spaniards, with fire and sword, saw to that, completing a massacre begun by the Maya themselves.

The Maya peasant even today is absolutely dependent upon the water supply for his crops; and his yearly round of work follows the seasons with the same great accuracy. In Yucatán, as in all areas of the Tropics, there are but two seasons, "dry" and "wet." In one, it rains; in the other, it doesn't. And the line of demarcation is almost as sharp as that. If the Maya is to live (and it is corn that forms three quarters of his diet even today), he must prepare and plant, harvest and store, in almost clock-like sequence.

With the exception of exchanging his stone celt for a steel ax, and a fire-hardened stick for an iron-pointed one, the Maya farmer cultivates land virtually as his ancestors did a thousand, two thousand, years ago.

After selecting a spot for his *milpa,* or cornfield, he chops down to ground level all its trees and brush. This is usually done during January, in order to permit it to dry out under the blazing suns of February and March. A field of ten or twelve acres is required for the feeding of a single family.

Come the appropriate day—and such a time was carefully studied and decreed by the ancient priests—usually in mid-March or April, the field is burned. Despite the fierce blaze, fanned by the wind, the surrounding jungle is not ignited; and the farmer ends with a neatly squared-off field for his crop.

Planting of the corn is done immediately after the first rains of the new season, which may come any time between April and July, but are traditionally expected on the Day of the Holy Cross (May 3). The farmer walks along, poking his sharp-pointed stick into the soil every four or five feet, and dropping half a dozen kernels into each hole. The farmer can now go away and relax, for in a newly cleared *milpa* he need weed only once during the growing season from May to September.

By the time September rolls around, his corn has grown and ripened with very little care from the farmer. But now he goes out and performs a most interesting act.

He cracks the stalks over so that the ears hang tassels down, permitting the rain to run off the sheltering husks.

When his corn has dried, perhaps in November, but principally in January and February, the crop is harvested, shelled, and stored. Now it is ready for eating and, always, a portion is laid aside at the outset for seed.

A *milpa* can only be used for two successive seasons, for beyond that time the weeds have sprung up so thickly that its yield is insufficient. The land is then allowed to return to jungle, and will be undisturbed for ten years before being once again cleared and the cycle renewed.

As you drive through the countryside of Yucatán you will see *milpas* in various stages of cultivation, and will recognize the swift takeover of the jungle as cleared areas disappear. (Considering this, it is amazing how well the Maya cities have withstood its grasp.)

The agricultural cycle played its part, too, in determining the size and duration of life of the Maya cities. For the peasant population not only had to support themselves, but priests and nobles as well. And, as the surrounding land lay fallow, longer and longer distances had to be covered to plant and pick the crops. Indeed, one cause of the disintegration of the cities of the Maya may well have been the exhaustion of the surrounding land.

Since the Mayan does not have to work overly hard to support his family, long periods of time are available to him—or to the priests and nobles who controlled his an-

cestors. The Maya cities, therefore, may actually have
been set up to keep the peasantry occupied—and to prevent them from thinking revolutionary thoughts against
their lords. This is another theory that has been advanced for the disintegration of the cities of the Maya:
that a peasant revolt utterly destroyed the ruling classes,
and, leaderless and mindless, the people decayed.

Consider this possibility. We know that throughout
the land of the Maya there existed a common form of
conventionalized priestly government. Could not a new
philosophy, an underground movement, have come into
being and erupted almost simultaneously over the land,
destroying that government and substituting anarchy?
There would no longer have been a reason for the existence of the great religious centers. We perhaps have lost
sight too readily of the fact that in the vast majority of
cases there were no Maya cities, but only ceremonial
centers. Without the priests that staffed and directed
them, there could come only disintegration and decay.
With the priests and nobles dead, the leaderless peasantry might scatter to their *milpas*, to remain leaderless
and subservient throughout the Spanish Conquest until
today.

The Spaniards came in search of gold and glory. They
found a hostile land, where each tribe they encountered
resisted them. Since the descriptions that are available
are those of the Spaniards themselves, they are not un-
prejudiced. We do not know with what subtle treachery
they met the Indians.

Regardless of where the virtue—if any—lies, the fact

remains that the Spaniards came to stay. They subdued the Mayan population, converted it to at least a nominal Catholicism, and took the land for themselves, reducing the Indians to peonage. Indeed, the conqueror of Chichén Itzá divided the towns and villages of the region among his soldiers, each Spaniard being allotted the services of twenty-five hundred Indians.

In the various Spanish expeditions that gradually took over Yucatán, a conquest that spread over only about thirty years, there are perhaps five names that are of particular interest: Gonzalez de Guerrero; Juan de Grijalva; Hernando Cortés (Mr. Conquistador himself); and the father and son Montejos.

Guerrero was part of a party shipwrecked in 1511 on the east coast of Yucatán. One of two survivors—the rest were said to be eaten by the Maya, although there is no other evidence of such a practice—he was caged to be fattened up for future feasts. Instead he secured his release into slavery, eventually drifting south to Chetumal. Here he entered the service of the king of that area, married his daughter, and rose to a powerful position. He later refused Cortés' offer of repatriation, choosing to spend his life with his Maya family. He obviously knew when he was well off.

Juan de Grijalva, in his expedition of 1518, followed the coast by ship south from the island of Cozumel. A notation from his sailing directions is the first description of Tulúm.

Cortés, of course, is a most familiar historical figure. He landed on Cozumel in 1519, destroying the idols in the temples that he found, and causing a cross to be erected in one of them. This is the famous Cozumel Cross, which was later moved to the Church of the Mejorada in Mérida, and now is in the Archaeological Museum in Mexico City. Cortés later sailed to Tabasco, reaching the seacoast near Villahermosa. Here he was given as a slave the famous Indian woman, La Malinche (The Tongue), whose knowledge of languages materially assisted in his conquest of Mexico. She came from the nearby town of Xicalanco, whose name means Place Where the Language Changes. This town was over the years the traditional meeting ground, trading place, and sanctuary between the tribes of the west—the Náhuatls, the Olmecs, the Toltecs—and the Maya of Yucatán. As such, it represented an important part in both the interchange of goods and of culture.

The conquest of Yucatán lasted for twenty years, from 1527 to 1546, and was actively directed by Don Francisco de Montejo, the father, and his son of the same name. They founded the first Ciudad Real (Royal City) at Chichén Itzá. Later the population revolted, but young Montejo succeeded in extricating his garrison by a ruse. He tied a dog to the clapper of a bell, and placed some food just out of his reach. The frantic ringing of the bell permitted the Spaniards to escape under cover of night.

In 1542, the Montejos founded "The Very Noble and Very Loyal City of Mérida," where you will find the house that they built in 1549 not only standing, but now inhabited by the fifteenth generation of the family of Montejo!

Why You Should
Go to Yucatán

This book is, of course, prejudiced: for it believes that there are innumerable reasons why Yucatán is *the* place to visit, reasons that focus principally on its beauty, its historical interest—and its archaeological mystery.

Indeed, the beauties, the history, and the riddle of Yucatán are the subject of this book. For as you drive through its miles of henequen plantations, enter its quaint, thatch-roofed villages immaculate in their white paint, and pass its golden Spanish churches, you suddenly come upon a towering pyramid, an intricately designed stone temple or palace, that rises a hundred feet or more above you, a wondrous relic of a civilization that sprang into being more than a thousand years ago—and as mysteriously disappeared, leaving city upon city of unsurpassed architectural beauty empty and deserted.

This, of course, is why you should go to Yucatán: to see for yourself wonders of beauty that rank equally with those the Old World has to offer, yet are almost at your front door. For the peninsula of Yucatán is near to us, just across the Gulf of Mexico, about 630 air miles from New Orleans, and only 700 from Miami. And if you happen to be in Mexico itself, Mérida, the central city of the peninsula, is less than 625 miles from Mexico City. So distance is no problem, as jets sweep in frequently to the long strip of Mérida airport.

Yucatán is a clean land, a land of friendly, cheerful people, where English is so much a third language (after Spanish and Mayan) that there is no problem for the traveler. It is, nonetheless, a foreign land, a place of excitingly different sights and sounds and smells, where women dress in their colorful *huipiles* and the *campesino* men carry a string bag, a machete, and a calabash drinking jug as naturally as you wear a coat and hat and carry an umbrella.

There are colorful fairs and fiestas, where the blue scent of copal incense hangs heavy in the air and drums beat a tantalizing rhythm. There are native markets, blocks square, where you can purchase—at bargain prices—almost anything under the sun. Fine baskets, or intricately handmade silver, an embroidered blouse or dress, a wonderfully comfortable native hammock, a Panama hat—you may look them over at your leisure, comparing prices and quality from stall to stall. Or if you do not wish to buy, but just look—or take photographs—there are vendors of brilliant red tomatoes, of shiny black *frijoles,* of golden oranges and green limes and yellow lemons, of fresh vegetables and fish, of spices and meats. And everywhere there are people, housewives carefully doing their daily marketing, *señoritas* from nearby stores and offices in their high heels and snug-fitting dresses, everywhere Maya Indians, shy and sweet and dignified in white dresses with horizontal bands of embroidered flowers.

You'll want to go to Yucatán just to sit in parks under the shade of great flamboyant trees and watch the world go by. Here is a native cart, very wide and flat, whose patient burro is driven by a cheerfully grinning young boy. Or tourists like yourself, but they have come all the way from Minnesota drawing their trailer home behind them to spend the winter or more under the kindly, warm sun. You'll find that they know a lot, too, about the local sights, for they have usually done a lot of reading up before they started their trek.

Look around the square while you relax. On one side there will be an old Spanish church, probably built in the 1500's. It will be much larger than would seem appropriate for the town, but it serves much of the surrounding countryside as well, and with labor from a virtual slave people, the ancient clergy were able to create little kingdoms for themselves. There will be stores, restaurants, and probably a pool hall, as well as government buildings on the other sides of the plaza; and, in Mérida, one of the loveliest buildings anywhere, the historic home of the Montejos with its plateresque facade.

But the glory that is Yucatán lives in the relics of the ancient Maya civilization a short distance from Mérida. In this land—a thousand years ago? five thousand years ago?—lived a people whose art and architecture must rank with those of the greatest of civilizations, yet the Maya culture ceased abruptly for a cause as yet unknown. Here are solid stone temples towering a hundred feet steeply above you, decorated with carvings of delicate beauty, yet which ceased to function for no apparent reason. Scowling, long-nosed masks glare down upon you, priests with feathered headdresses offer a dignified, stone-carved sacrifice; fierce warriors by thousands prance in battle array; an eagle tears at a human heart in its talons; and a cold-visaged, impersonal Chac Mool awaits his virginal sacrifice. These sights will fascinate you in the land of the Maya.

Come to Yucatán? You must!

What You Should
See in Yucatán

If your first response is "Maya ruins," you may well be so
uninterested that you will never come to Yucatán. For
few sights are so uninspiring as cluttered piles of gray
stone. And this is especially true if you do not know how
the stones happened to be there in the first place.

The real response, then, is "Maya cities," and the
more you know of their background the more you will
appreciate their beauty. For to you these will not be
mounds of stone, but temples and palaces, stadia and ob-
servatories—places where people lived and worked and
worshiped.

You will see a pyramid in Chichén Itzá, towering a
hundred feet in the air to culminate in a majestic
temple; and you will know that hidden in its interior is
still another temple containing "the most outstanding
archaeological object ever discovered in the New
World," the Red Jaguar Throne, with its eyes and its
spots of green jade. And for your greater appreciation

you will know the significance of the jaguar and the part it played in the life of the city.

You will see a stadium, roughly the size of a football field, where the outcome of the game meant life or death to the participants. And you will realize why this was so, why the ancient fertility rite demanded death as a basis for life.

You will see a circular tower where in ancient times priests kept their night-long vigils to mark the spot of the instant of sunrise. And you will know that it was these priests, more than two thousand years ago, who were able to calculate the length of our year with such great exactitude that they foreshadowed our own present calendar.

You will see a long building in Uxmal crowning a man-made hilltop where each one of the twenty thousand stones that forms its façade was so carefully placed as to be part of a pattern, to develop an endless chiaroscuro of light and shade. And you will wonder at the height of the development of art and architecture that made this beauty possible.

Nearby you will see a two-headed, conjoined jaguar couched in majesty on a platform, staring proudly across acres of lawn. And you will recognize it as a marriage symbol, for the banded sides show the eternal union of man and wife.

In Palenque you will climb down a narrow stairway into a *subterráneo* and, by the light of a match, you will see carved into the stone lintel above you the exquisite form of a kneeling priestess, her hands stretched out in perpetual prayer. Not many people will have seen her before you, for since the time she was first chiseled out and left forgotten, early explorers failed to notice this sculpture.

You will see a cross, stretching out its arms on a pagan altar, to which majestic priests made solemn offering— while standing on the backs of kneeling slaves. And you will know the legend that tells of a bearded white man in a white robe who came to Yucatán almost two millennia ago to bring a new religion to the people of the land of the Maya.

You may even crawl down into a cave—do not be afraid, for it opens to soaring heights over your head— and see where stalactite and stalagmite have joined to form an underground altar; and see, exactly as they were left there by worshipers six centuries ago, their votive offerings to the gods of tne land: Chac, the omnipresent Maya God of Rain; and Tláloc, the mustachioed Toltec divinity. Very, very few people have been here, although it is located close to Chichén Itzá, for it was only discovered by accident in 1959, and only recently opened to visitors.

You will see a temple of golden limestone at Dzibilchaltún, rising delicately out of mile upon mile of gray-green henequen spikes. And you will anxiously await a closer view, for you know that it was built over 1,500 years ago, the focal point of a city of 125,000 people. Below its altar, leading into a crypt, is a tube to enable the priests to communicate with the souls of the dead. You will marvel at its beauty, and you will thrill to its mystery.

And these are only a few of the sights that you will see in the land of the ancient Maya. The more you see, the more you understand of the civilization that made them possible, the greater will be your enjoyment and appreciation of the Maya cities.

Where You Should Go— and for How Long

The central point for any trip within Yucatán is the city of Mérida, a clean, bustling metropolis of some two hundred thousand people, with excellent hotels, restaurants, and facilities for visitors. Whether you fly in from the United States or from Mexico City, Mérida will be your headquarters. Chichén Itzá, Dzibilchaltún, and Uxmal are all easily accessible from here, as are the Spanish cities of Izamal, Valladolid, and Progreso.

You will enjoy Mérida, for there is much for you to do and see while you are in the city. It has beautiful parks, lovely ancient churches, the magnificent Montejo house, and an excellent archaeological museum.

The best way to appreciate your visit to Yucatán is to allow a day's stay in Mérida for sightseeing before setting out for the Maya cities, and at least another day there between your visits to Chichén Itzá and Uxmal.

How long you should stay is, of course, a highly personal question, determined by the time you have made available. It is possible to "do" Yucatán in three or four days; most people will spend a week to ten days. And at least a week is recommended.

Why hurry? You'll find that the more you know about a place, the longer you'll want to stay there. As you look, the first thing you'll want to do is to see it as a whole, one structure in relation to another, with grassy sweeps of lawn in between. Then you'll want to look at the architecture itself, the form of the buildings, the beauty of their proportions. Next you'll note the details, the frets, the meanders, the undulating lines. Only then will you appreciate the meaning of each of these elements that you have seen: the serpents, the jaguars, the tortoises, the tears on the nose of Chac. Now you will have really seen the relics of the Mayan civilization. You will have gained a deep and lasting appreciation of what you have seen, and you will have enjoyed yourself to the full. Can you achieve this in a day or so?

Plan to see Yucatán at a leisurely and appreciative pace. Enjoy yourself! Try this schedule:

1ST DAY   P.M.   Arrive in Mérida and get your bearings.

2ND DAY   A.M.   Take a carriage drive around town.

              P.M.   See the Cathedral, Montejo house, and Plaza Mayor.

3RD DAY   A.M.   Drive to Chichén Itzá, lunching at Valladolid.

              P.M.   Take a first look at Chichén Itzá's North Area.

4TH DAY   A.M.   Visit the North Area.

          P.M.   Visit the Central Area. (Spend an-
                 other day—or two—here if you can,
                 visiting "Old Chichén" and the Cave
                 of Balancanche, and revisiting some
                 of your favorite places at a more
                 leisurely pace.)

5TH DAY   A.M.   Take a last look at Chichén Itzá and
                 lunch at your hotel.

          P.M.   Return to Mérida via Izamal.

6TH DAY   A.M.   Drive to Dzibilchaltún, lunching in
                 Progreso.

          P.M.   Return to Mérida, visit the museum.

7TH DAY   A.M.   Drive to Uxmal and have lunch at
                 your hotel.

          P.M.   Take a look at Uxmal.

8TH DAY   A.M. ⎫
               ⎬ Visit the buildings of Uxmal.
          P.M. ⎭

          Safari to Kabáh, Sayil, Labná, and
          X-lapahk. (Spend another day in
9TH DAY   A.M. Uxmal if you can, revisiting the
          P.M. buildings for the architectural detail
          here is especially beautiful and mean-
          ingful.)

10TH DAY A.M.   Return to the sites of Uxmal once
                 more before leaving for Mérida.

P.M.   Have lunch at your hotel in Mérida
and then visit the market area.

11TH DAY   A.M.   Leave Mérida.

Admittedly, this still will leave you with a lot unseen.
But now that you know of the beauties that lie so near,
you'll want to return to Yucatán.

Where You Should Stay—
and Dine

This is definitely not a book on how to travel on $5 or even $10 a day, nor is it a guide (if such a thing is possible!) for the jet set. Instead, it assumes that you are a person of intelligence, and that, whether you are eighteen or eighty-five (or anywhere in between) you enjoy and appreciate new experiences.

Of equal importance to where you stay, then, is what you eat and drink. Luckily, there is no dearth of fine accommodations and excellent food and beverages throughout Yucatán. You may, therefore, reasonably lay aside such worries as often beset even the experienced traveler, and enjoy yourself in Mérida and in the facilities offered at the Maya sites. You may assume that those listed below are consonant with the standards you are accustomed to in the United States. Not, heaven forbid, that they will be carbon copies—for each has its own ambience—but that they will meet your best expectations in quality of accommodations, service, and food.

In MÉRIDA, you will probably want to stay at the Hotel Panamericana or the Hotel Mérida. The former is newer, and contains the offices of the Barbachano Travel Bureau, the major agency serving the Yucatán Peninsula.

If you stay at the HOTEL PANAMERICANA, try to get a room high up, on the fifth or sixth floor, for the lower ones are apt to be filled with music from the orchestra that plays nightly (until midnight) around the pool-bar-terrace. All rooms, by the way, are air-conditioned, so if you like this modern monstrosity, you'll be pretty well soundproofed. If you are high up, ask for a room facing the pool (*a frente de la piscina*), for the view over the city is beautiful. Rooms facing the street (Calle 59) are quieter, but your room can get pretty hot from the afternoon sun. Be sure to look carefully at the lobby and patio of the hotel, for it was a part of an original Victorian mansion, and the stucco reliefs on the cornices are fully the equal of those found anywhere else. Even if you are not staying at this hotel make it a point to come to see these decorations; for, with their white doves flying in almost full relief against the deep crimson background, they are a magnificent piece of artistry.

The principal problem of the Hotel Panamericana is that it is not too central (but since many Americans choose to ride when they can walk, this may not be a bother, as taxis and *calesas*—horse-drawn carriages—are readily available). Parking facilities are excellent, and both Hertz and Avis rental offices are located here.

The HOTEL MÉRIDA has a better location—Calle 60.

Two blocks from the Parque Cepada and four from the Plaza Mayor, it provides a wonderful opportunity for an after-dinner stroll. Nights are cool—just right—so you'll enjoy your evening *paseo*.

There are a number of good places to eat in Mérida. You will like the Panamericana's dining room, open to the gentle breeze. Its food is good and simple, and perhaps it would be the best place to eat upon your arrival, when you are still all excited from your trip.

The elegant place in town is the RÉAL MONTEJO, a taxi ride away near the *Alameda*. Go into the back dining room, through the glass doors in the rear by the bar. The service there is better, and there is greater attention to detail.

The best food, however, is certainly at the CONTI-NENTAL, a few blocks out on Calle 57 from the Hotel Mérida. It is owned and run by Lebanese, is much frequented by Mexicans, and, while its approach (and prices) is simpler than that of the Réal Montejo, there is greater attention given to the preparation of the varied selection of food.

You'll probably want to try, too, LOS TULIPANES, which is located on the edge of the city proper, outdoors, beside a huge *cenote* (subterranean pool). Take a *calesa* to get there, and enjoy the jogging gait. The driver, for a small fee (agreed upon in advance), will wait outside while you eat. It's quite gay in the evenings, and you will be interested to walk down to the cave of the *cenote*, now used as a swimming pool by local families.

The MIRADOR, atop the Hotel Mérida, is seasonally

open only on Saturday evenings. Unfortunately, dining out in Mexico is so late that you won't have a chance to watch the sunset, but Mérida's answer to "The Top of the Mark" affords a lovely view of the lights of the city spread below; food and service are fine.

In CHICHÉN ITZÁ, the HOTEL MAYALAND is more luxurious than the HACIENDA CHICHÉN; it is, in fact, a deluxe hotel by any standards. See if you can arrange to stay in a little *casita* there. These small, thatch-roofed Mayan houses (each with private bath and twin beds) are scattered about the grounds, connected with the attractive main hotel by cement walks. Most are two-family affairs, but the one nearest the hotel you can have all to yourself, and it's just lovely, with its encircling porch where you may sit and rest and read, or have your evening cocktail. Stay away from the new wing if at all possible, it's too near the road. This hotel is American Plan, and food and service are excellent. After dinner you can watch a bit of native dancing (the *jalapa*), performed by various waiters and waitresses, and be offered a free glass of Mayan liqueur (Xtabentun), made from honey and flavored with anise. All create a very colorful and relaxing backdrop for going to bed early, since sightseeing is active!

At UXMAL, it's the HACIENDA UXMAL, quite similar to the Mayaland, and just as nice. Here the best rooms are on the second floor of the wing that stretches to the north, behind the swimming pool. Again, avoid if at all possible the new construction, which borders on the highway. (Why, with thousands of square miles of jungle around, the building had to be situated alongside a road where buses roar by, announcing their coming with long-drawn-out, train-like hoots is a mystery that, probably, no American will ever solve.) The attraction at the Hacienda Uxmal is a group of native crafts shops selling well-made and -designed earthenware, bags, embroidery, and silver. These objects are made by local Indians in huts near the swimming pool, and you may enjoy watching them at work.

In the proposed itinerary, the suggestion was made that you might enjoy lunching at VALLADOLID. This simple, pleasant old Spanish town is situated a dozen miles past Chichén Itzá. While not worth extending your trip to see, if you leave Mérida after breakfast, Valladolid is a very "different" place to lunch in native, rather than tourist, surroundings. The restaurant is called the CENOTE ZACÍ, and you will eat in a large thatched hut looking down into the pool of the *cenote*. After your lunch (*arroz con pollo*—rice with chicken—and *cerveza* —beer—is recommended), you can walk down a path just above the water, looking up at the overhanging cave edge with its stalactites and rim of green vines. By lunching here on your first day, and at the hotel in Chichén Itzá prior to your departure for Izamal, you'll round out two full American Plan days. There is, unfortunately, no recommended restaurant in Izamal.

On another day, that of your trip to Dzibilchaltún, lunch at PROGRESO is suggested. The HOTEL COCOTEROS is not in Progreso itself, but about four miles east along the coast, in an infinitesimal town of that name. It is a simple place, with no pretensions of attracting the tourist trade, but the fish is superb, practically still flapping, it's so fresh. Don't concern yourself with the species, just have *pescado*—or, if you have a choice, try the *huachinango* (red snapper). Start your lunch with the fish soup, a vegetable broth using fish stock. Dessert? Grapefruit (*torjona*—or *pómelo,* if available).

What You Should Eat— and Drink

You should have few, if any, problems with foods and beverages in Yucatán. You will be staying and eating at places where catering to non-Mexican tastes and customs is a part of the normal service, and so you can, within reason, eat or drink anything that is served to you.

Of course, any rapid change of climate, time zone, or diet is likely to disturb your digestion; so it is suggested that you stick to the simpler things for a day or two until you become fully acclimatized.

A few routine questions always arise. How about the water? is probably the most common. The Hotel Mayaland and the Hacienda Uxmal both have their own wells, and their water is completely safe to drink and use. Elsewhere, stick to bottled water, although most restaurants serve *agua purificada,* which is perfectly satisfactory. If you're in any doubt, buy bottled water. And don't forget that ice is only frozen water, and if you don't drink the water you shouldn't put ice in your drink.

Salads? Again, the Mayaland and the Hacienda Uxmal both have their own vegetable gardens, so you may eat what is put before you; but away from there you should avoid salads. After all, you are in Yucatán to enjoy yourself to the full, and you don't want to be uncomfortable.

Fruits? Delicious and safe at any of the major hotels. Away from them, avoid anything you don't peel yourself. Fruit juices, particularly orange (*jugo de naranja nativa*) may be readily enjoyed.

Milk? Not recommended. While pasteurization plants do exist, there is no assurance that your particular glass of milk will be processed as it would be in the States. Cream? It probably is condensed milk, and hence safe . . . but how about drinking your coffee black for a week or so? You might even get to like it that way. Butter? Like the cream, it's probably a substitute, margarine. If it isn't, it's canned from Denmark or New Zealand, and a mite strong-tasting, but it won't hurt you.

As to foods, the first thing you'll probably be happy to know is that the Yucatecans don't go in for "hot" (*picante*), peppery, spicy dishes. Your meats will be more seasoned than you are accustomed to, but you won't burn your mouth out or gasp for breath after each bite. So you need not hesitate about tackling typically Yucatecan dishes, and you'll find many of them on menus wherever you go.

At dinner, your choices may run to something like the following, which will at least give you some idea of what to expect.

Appetizer. Choice of shrimp (*camarónes*) or abalone (concha), or, possibly, *seviche.* The last is raw fish, flaked and marinated in coconut milk and lime juice. It's very digestible and tasty, although some places have a tendency to add a spot of Tabasco to the marinade. The abalone, or conch, is cooked, and although it looks like small bits of rubber, is more tender than you would expect. The shrimp are superb in Mérida or on the coast, but they don't travel too well. There is a tiny variety from Campeche that are, as the city's Chamber of Commerce says, "the best shrimp in the world." They have much the same flavor as Dublin Bay prawns, but are even more delicate and sea-y. So your dinner has started out well.

Soup. Generally this will be a genuine *pot au feu,* where a caldron simmers on the back of the stove, and the rich stock is mixed with vegetables. Especially recommended on the seacoast is the fish soup, a sort of Manhattan fish chowder with tomatoes that really brings you the taste of the sea. And it's not too filling.

Main courses. You will usually have available three choices. And now you might as well learn of a minor failing in Yucatecan cooking. They love onions, and use them excessively. But it really is a minor failing, for they can be readily combed out of the sauce so that you can enjoy the dish itself.

The first selection will be between either fish or shrimp or eggs. The variety of fish (*pescado*) is relatively unimportant, for fish in the tropical waters don't get enough exercise and so all tend to taste pretty much alike. But there are red snapper and *mero* (sea trout), among others. Abalone or conch might turn up in this course as well as shrimp, cooked in a variety of ways. And you may be so lucky as to find listed *calamares en su tinta* (octopus or squid cooked in its own ink . . . no, not "Ugh!" but delicious). It's really very good: tender and not at all strong-tasting.

The second selection will be either chicken or turkey, cooked in an infinite variety of ways—all of them good. If you want a "native" dish, try *pollo pibil,* a sort of mildly barbecued chicken cooked in banana leaves. *Arroz con pollo* is a standby. No matter where you get it, it will always be tasty, even if, sometimes, the chicken is an old gentleman who has seen far too much service. In season, you'll find *pato* (duck), not the barnyard variety, but wild duck, usually teal. It is cooked the way we cook regular duck, though it has a delicate gamy flavor.

Game is plentiful in Yucatán, and you will almost always find venison (*venado*) as a possibility among the red meats. Its best incarnation is possibly *pibian de venado,* venison cooked in a pumpkin-like sauce that makes a superb and very different stew. Speaking of stews, if you see *carne de res* (beef) listed, you'll do well to select some other dish, since steers are likely to have gotten pretty tough before they attained slaughtering age.

Vegetables. Fresh greens are so scarce as to be nonexistent. Such greens as there are come out of cans. There are two types of summer squash you will frequently find listed, *calabaza* and *chayote,* both slightly watery, harmless, and uninteresting. You'll do far better always to have *frijoles*. These are black beans mashed and served in an unattractive puddle, with bits of toasted *tortillas* sticking out of them to use as edible forks. Actually they are very pleasant tasting, and are an almost perfectly balanced food, composing the staple diet for millions of Central Americans. If you should find them unappetizing in the first place you try them, do not be discouraged, for every cook seems to have a slightly different way of preparing them, and some methods are a lot better than others. The same holds true in the case of another standard vegetable, *plátanos fritos* (fried bananas). Some like to use the fruit while relatively green (in Panama they even slice it very thin and serve it with cocktails, like potato chips); others prefer to use a ripe red banana, and fry it quite lightly, leaving it soft and succulent. But you'll never know in advance which you are going to be served.

Tortillas are, of course, a standard Mexican food. Made from corn and toasted, they are simply delicious, and may be procured anywhere. In fact, you will find that at the private *haciendas* or *fincas* there is a woman whose only function is to prepare *tortillas*, a task that keeps her time fully occupied. And John Lloyd Stephens, on his fascinating trip to Yucatán in 1840— that's right, 1840—while he was living in the Governor's Palace at Uxmal, had Chaipa Chi, a native woman who did nothing else but make *tortillas*.

Breads. Your guide to Yucatán would not be complete without mention of the delicious local breads. While lacking the character of the Irish homemade breads, the white breads of Yucatán are always fresh and moist, and will generally be prepared as French rolls. Don't worry about the butter that you are not going to eat with them, for they're excellent just plain. Or you can have them with *mermelada,* a term that embraces all types of jam, so you'll have to specify the type of fruit: *mermelada de naranja* (orange marmalade) or *mermelada de fresas* (strawberry jam). Be sure to appreciate to the full the Yucatecan honey. It is quite brown, relatively thin in consistency, and with a slightly bitter aftertaste. (Those of you who have bought some good lady's "wildflower honey" at a church fair in the South will know exactly what this means.) Curiously enough, when you ask that honey be served you (although the dictionary word for honey is *miel*), you'll have to specify *miel de abeja* (honey of the bee) to distinguish it from such *Yanqui* imports as *miel de maple* (maple syrup) and even *miel de Karo!*

Desserts. The one that is the most *típico* and universally available is *flan,* caramel custard. Unfortunately, it can be prepared in a variety of ways, ranging from palatable (out of a package) to superb; and there is no way of knowing in advance which you will be getting. But it's always worth the try: when it's good, it's very, very good. Fruits are, of course, a favorite after a plentiful meal; and there is nothing like a papaya just fully ripe (*muy maduro*) with a squeeze of lime on it. Its deep orange color is a delight to behold, and it has a very delicate melon flavor, not at all ammoniac like some cantaloupes.

Beverages. As an afterthought, it is well worth knowing that Decaf (decaffeinated coffee by Nestlé) is widely available. But if you are one who must have a cup of decaffeinated coffee wherever you go, buy a small jar or some packets in the States and carry them with you just to make sure.

Now, as to what to drink with your meal. Yucatecan beers are very good. The light ones are more robust than some of ours, but you'll enjoy their lightness and flavor. A number of brands are sold, and your tastebuds will be your best guide, but Carta Clara is a leader. If your tastes are a bit more esoteric, don't miss Leon Negra, a very dark-colored beer that has much of the taste of Guinness stout. Like Guinness, too, it is low in effervescence, making it a deeply thirst-quenching drink. There are other *cervezas oscuras* (dark beers), and you may well end up by having made a discovery of how delicious such a beer can be.

Mexican wines are generally satisfactory, even though their taste is not quite what your palate might expect. The brand most commonly distributed in Yucatán seems to be Alamo, which is certainly the peer of those found elsewhere. To get the very best in any brand of Mexican wine, be sure that the word "extra" is on the label. For example, there is a *Vino Blanco Extra—Alamo Seco,* which compares most favorably with a really good French Chablis; and there is also *Alamo Seco,* not quite so dry and clean-tasting, but very pleasant drinking nonetheless. The rosés, sometimes called *rosados,* are more grapey than you will be accustomed to, even sometimes almost resembling a muscatel. The clarets, which really aren't, have very much of a wild-grape flavor ("foxy" is the wine taster's term), and, once you accept that fact, make delicious accompaniment to the red meats.

The liqueur indigenous to Yucatán is Xtabentun, a clear anise-flavored drink made from honey. You may want to take some home with you as a "different" souvenir. The Mexican liqueur now becoming quite well known in the States is Kahlua. It is made from coffee, and is delicious.

There is certainly one other typically Yucatecan drink that you should enjoy: hot chocolate. While generally available, it is especially pleasant to sit at a small table at the Café Expres on Mérida's Parque Cepada and look at the *calesas* standing there while you have your *chocolate hecho con agua* (made with water). You can even walk to the rear of the counter and watch your drink being made. The ground cocoa bean is mixed with boiling water and whipped with wooden paddles until it dissolves. You then add sugar to your taste, or perhaps you'll prefer it in its natural, rather pleasantly bitter state. Since you are trying to avoid milk, be sure to mention the *agua,* although either liquid makes a delicious beverage.

What You Should Wear

Clothing is a problem at any time or place, especially since traveling by air compels you to restrict your wardrobe. Fortunately, Yucatán is a simple place and you can keep your packing to a minimum.

The ladies, because they seem to have the most problems—or at any rate to worry about them more—will have to plan for three activities: daytime wear in the city of Mérida, "pyramid-climbing" at the Maya cities, and evening wear.

What to wear in Mérida is accompanied by a prohibition: do *not* wear slacks or shorts. Period. As an experienced traveler, you may well already know this Latin American (and Continental) fact of life; but too many think it's all right—and it isn't. So wear a simple daytime dress, preferably drip-dry and crease-resistant, such as you would consider appropriate in any small southern town or city, perhaps a "shift" or a skirt and blouse. Shoes should be low-heeled, for even if you do your city sightseeing by *calesa,* you'll still want to get out on occasion for a closer or more extensive look, and high heels can be difficult to manage on rough, uneven surfaces. Carry a scarf or "chapel-cap" in your bag, for there are many lovely churches you will want to enter—to see the architecture and possibly to say a brief prayer.

When it comes to "pyramid-climbing" (and this includes all sightseeing at the Maya cities, even if you never ascend a pyramid) slacks are just the thing! You, as an experienced traveler, may not have realized that custom could give way to utility! Shorts are still out, except for the young and slender. As to slacks, you'll probably want to wear something slim and lovely; but if you are really going to enjoy the magnificence of the sites, you're going to want to climb pyramids; and you will be wise to wear casual slacks or blue jeans so that you can relax and not worry about what might happen to your Pucci pants! The pyramids are steep, the stone is rough, and the steps are sandy: so put on what is suitable. Blue jeans are excellent, because they are tough, don't show stains, and have tight cuffs that won't catch on your shoes. Sneakers are advisable (some people even wear the heavier boat shoes, for an added feeling of secure grip), but any well-fitting, heel-less shoe is fine—just as long as you're comfortable in it.

Evenings are no problem at all. You and everyone else will be happily tired after a day of sightseeing, whether in Mérida or at the Maya cities, and all you'll need is a simple cocktail dress. If you care whether people see you twice in the same dress, bring a few. But neither you nor your friends will be concerned with what you're wearing, for you'll be far too interested in exchanging your exciting experiences, and reliving your wonderful day. Be sure, though, to bring along a light evening sweater or wrap (maybe you'll buy a Mexican shawl—a *rebozo*), since the temperature drops fast after sundown, and the sun sets early.

Men have only two wardrobe problems, day and evening; for if you are traveling as lightly as possible (to allow for purchases as well as your wife's "extras"), you can wear the same clothing in Mérida that you will in your pyramid-climbing.

In the daytime, slacks and a sports shirt are fine throughout Yucatán. If you want variety, wear lightweight slacks in Mérida and khakis for pyramid-climbing. The latter are highly recommended if you tend to be adventurous in your exploring and less careful of your things. In any event, you don't want to have to pay attention to your clothes when there are so many exciting sights. Sneakers for you too, if possible also with non-slip soles, are suggested, but once again comfort is the thing. All footwear takes a bit of a beating from the edges of the pyramid steps, so why not get something at a discount house, instead of an expensive pair?

In the evening, unfortunately, you'll find that many men do not wear coats or ties. You should. There is a reason for this paradox. Mexicans very frequently dine out (especially a group of men together) wearing slacks and a *guayabera* (a white cotton or linen coat-like shirt with various decorative pleats and buttons). You will undoubtedly want to bring one home—they are ideal for informal summer wear. The *guayabera* comes in two forms, either a short Eisenhower jacket, or a longer model with squared-off tails. Both are worn *outside* the trousers for coolness. The shirt is left open at the neck. So if a Mexican can dine out at a restaurant—properly attired—in an open-neck shirt, how can the manager tell a happy American in a sports shirt that he isn't properly dressed? As you can understand, then, you should either wear a light jacket and tie or follow Mexican styles.

For both sexes, light, broad-brimmed straw hats are advised, for the sun can be very hot and burning if you are not accustomed to it. A lightweight raincoat is also wise to have along, although you probably won't have it with you when you need it, for showers come and, as swiftly, go. However, should a *norte* hit, not only will the temperature drop steeply and a strong wind blow, but it will be accompanied by a driving cold rain that may last all day.

What the Weather Is Like

There are actually about as many opinions about the weather in Yucatán as there are people who inquire about it. The most valid response is "not cold." Around noon, at its peak, the thermometer will reach well into the 80's, but the nights cool off pleasantly for sleeping, and you'll welcome a light sweater or a jacket on your evening stroll.

The dry season officially commences with the month of March, but February has mostly sunny days with an occasional brief shower.

The real joker in the weather of Yucatán is the *norte,* the chilling winds that sweep cold Canadian air all the way across the Gulf of Mexico: it can drop the temperature 20° in a matter of minutes. What's more, a *norte* can last several days, thus being a relative of our New England three-day "nor'easters." In this case, however, once the front has passed the weather clears, but the wind continues to blow—and blow—and blow; and not just blow, but howl. There is no protection against it, and you'll just have to sit it out and not let it interfere too much with your sightseeing.

There are also *pequeños* (little) *nortes,* where clouds come, and the wind builds up a bit, and there may be a little rain. But these are really not bothersome, for they do not last long.

But every place has vagaries of its weather. The Virgin Islands have their "Christmas winds"—which visitors in March are told are "continuing unusually long this year"! And with your raincoat, and the prospect of a hot bath afterward, you need not become discouraged. Hint: take a bath towel and wrap it like a scarf around your neck.

Helpful Hints

Tipping. This is generally no problem if you let the *pesos* be your standard of thinking, and tip proportionately the same as you do in the States. For example, if your restaurant check (*la cuenta*) runs to $130 *mn* (that translates as 130 pesos—*mn* means *moneda nacional,* not "Mexican"), for dinner, including your bottle of wine, and you usually tip 15 percent, you'll leave the waiter 20 pesos. It is not recommended that you go above the 15 percent level in Yucatán.

If you are staying American Plan—and you will at both the Hotel Mayaland and the Hacienda Uxmal—allow about 20 pesos per day per couple for the waitress; plus, for a three-day stay, another 10–15 pesos for the entire time for the headwaiter (or waitress). Tip as you leave, not daily. At the Mayaland, your waitress will follow you from table to table, wherever you may happen to be seated, and you will tip her directly. At the Hacienda Uxmal, you will give the proper sum to the headwaiter, who puts it into a pool.

Bellboys and porters at hotels and airports should get about 1 peso per bag.

You will frequently find a man in a semi-uniform (some sort of cap with badge), who has a parking concession in places that we would consider to be free city parking. He is an official "car watcher," and expects about 1 peso an hour.

Taxis are privately operated, and drivers are usually not given a tip in addition to their fare, unless they perform some special service. All taxi rates should be settled in advance, since there are no meters or set fares. For example, 15 to 20 pesos to or from the Mérida airport is about right.

Since people work to earn money, they naturally like to be well tipped. But you, as an experienced traveler, can sense an undercurrent of resentment when some stupid person treats pesos as "funny money" and throws them around. Mexicans—in fact, every nationality in the world—are proud people who do not like to feel that their country is in any way being demeaned.

Tip about 3 pesos to the boy who brings you your ice, If you are going to have cocktails on your porch. Tip the barber about what you would in the States; if your haircut costs 10 pesos, give 2 or 3. This same scale applies to ladies at beauty parlors. (Incidentally, the best is at the Hotel Mérida, and a very good one it is.) You'll end up by tipping about 33 percent, about 8 pesos on a 22-peso bill. If you are in doubt as to who should receive how much, just ask the proprietress.

Keep plenty of change with you at all times. It will

stop you from tipping unnecessarily high. The 1-peso pieces are about the size and weight of the half dollar, making them a lot to lug around; but there are 1-peso bills, too.

Duty-free liquor. Before you leave the airport in the States, go to the international duty-free liquor shop. American or Scotch whiskies are expensive in Mexico, and this shop will deliver yours to your plane, not included as part of your luggage weight. How much you are allowed to bring in varies with government regulations, but the store will have the latest information.

Health precautions. If, as suggested, you watch your diet, you should have no trouble with the *turistas* (*diarrhea*), but just in case, take a bottle of Donnagel-PG or Paregoric along with you. You'll find that some of your friends will recommend Enterovioform, but that's really a specific for amebic dysentery, and if you get that you should be in a doctor's hands anyway. Besides, with increasing cleanliness and knowledge of sanitation, the possibilities of picking up this "bug" are remote, for you'll be staying at and eating in places where ample precautions will be taken.

A spray can of insect repellent should be packed. Not that you will find yourself beset by bugs—the areas are remarkably well controlled—but there are two places where it will be needed. One is if you walk to "Old Chichén." In preparation, spray yourself thoroughly, especially from the waist down. (The desk at the Hotel Mayaland will delegate a bellboy to spray you with their DDT when they learn you are taking this walk.) As you

walk, stay in the middle of the cleared path and try not
to brush against twigs or grass. This is a precaution
against *garrapatas,* a type of tick. You can get rid of them
by taking a bath, but you don't want to get them on you
if you can possibly avoid it, for you will itch like the
devil. Don't let this advice discourage you from going to
"Old Chichén," though. Just take normal precautions,
and all will be well. *Garrapatas* are found wherever ani-
mals are, so if you do much walking around back in the
Labná-Sayil area, you might as well spray some on there,
too. Beyond these specific places, you'll have no problems.

Air travel. Be sure to *reconfirm* any airline reserva-
tions as soon as you arrive, and then check again the day
before departure to make certain. Departing flights seem
to have a way of getting overbooked anyway, so try to be
among the first out to the airport, even if it does seem to
be unnecessarily early, and get into line until you have
your boarding pass in your hand.

If you are booked tourist, and your luggage turns out
to be substantially overweight, consider shifting to first
class. The difference isn't substantial, and you get wonderful comfort, fine food (the steak, on Pan American,
cooked to your order, is literally out of this world!) and
excellent wines; so you can convince yourself you are
really just buying a very fine meal!

Taking pictures. As you travel through the countryside you will find that many people are reluctant to pose
for pictures. This is a genuine feeling of reluctance and
is based on the fact that they are not wearing their best

clothes for such an important occasion. You cannot convince them that they are picturesque dressed as they are. So do not try. In other words, don't treat people as scenery. Do not use flashbulbs or bulky, conspicuous equipment in churches, unless you have secured permission from and are accompanied by the padre. And do not take pictures of people at worship.

What You Should Read

The Ancient Maya, by Sylvanus Griswold Morley, revised by George W. Brainerd. Stanford University Press, 3rd Edition, 1956. 507 pages, $8.50.

The definitive book on the subject. Really a college textbook, it is sometimes a bit heavy going, but if you want the facts, this is your basic reference. Excellent illustrations and maps.

The Maya, by Michael D. Coe. Frederick A. Praeger, 1966. 252 pages, $7.50.

A new book by an eminent authority, scholarly yet readable. You will be interested in the conclusions that the author reaches as he ties the Mayas in with the other Meso-American civilizations. (Another in this series, *Mexico,* by the same author, is also well worth reading.)

An Introduction to American Archaeology, by Gordon R. Willey, Volume I, "North and Middle America." Prentice-Hall, Inc., 1966. 526 pages, $16.95.

A lengthy chapter on Meso-America covers the whole

story of the Maya from the jungles of the Petén to the limestone hills of the Puuc, the rain forests of Chiapas and the mountains of Pacific Guatemala. A lavishly illustrated, beautifully turned-out book by a recognized leader in the field.

Incidents of Travel in Yucatán, by John Lloyd Stephens. Now in Dover paperback, 2 volumes. 639 pages, $4.00.

A completely enchanting story of the author's travels in his search for Maya cities a hundred and twenty-five years ago. (He found them, too, probably more than anyone else has seen since.) Magnificently illustrated by engravings by his friend and traveling companion, Frederick Catherwood. You will be charmed by this book, for it is not only a classic of travel and exploration, and, as such, scientifically well informed, but it is a lively and delightful description of the land, its people and its customs.

Incidents of Travel in Central America, Chiapas and Yucatán, by John Lloyd Stephens, illustrated by Frederick Catherwood. Rutgers University Press, 1949. 747 pages, $10.00.

If you get bitten by "the Stephen's bug" you'll want to have this too, although he only reaches Palenque and Uxmal toward the end of his trip through the area. But excitement seems to follow the man wherever he travels, and he tells a wonderful tale!

Temples in Yucatán, by Laura Gilpin. Hastings House, 1948. 124 pages, $5.95.

This "camera chronicle" is a *must* as a souvenir of your trip, and is a valuable aid in visualizing what you are about to see as well. (Better get it while it is still in print.) Her photographs of Chichén Itzá are lovely, and her descriptive text pleasant, if not necessarily archaeologically exact.

An Album of Maya Architecture, by Tatiana Proskouriakoff. University of Oklahoma Press, 1963. 142 pages, $7.95.

This fascinating series of drawings was first published (in a larger page size) by the Carnegie Institution of Washington. Full-page illustrations show various Maya sites as Miss Proskouriakoff imagines them, in the full flower of their culture. Since she has not only great artistic ability coupled with architectural training, but is also a most competent archaeologist, the results are most inspiring. Additionally, smaller facing illustrations show the site as it presently exists, so you can do your own reconstruction. The accompanying text is sound and readable.

The World of the Maya, by Victor W. von Hagen. New American Library (Mentor Book), 1960. 224 pages, $.75.

A popularized version of the complete story of the Maya. Yet still pretty heavy reading, and not as sound as Morley, Coe or Willey. More concerned with Maya life than with the details of their cities. Illustrated but inadequately so.

Maya Cities, by Paul Rivet. Published by Elek-Putnam. Translated from the French in 1960. 234 pages. $5.95.

Lavishly illustrated, but with a great many sights you'll never see (and the author didn't either!). A lovely book for your living-room table, but not as a reference aid.

Official Guides are published by the Instituto Nacional de Antropologia e Historia. English editions available as listed from the Institute at Cordoba 45, Mexico City 7, D.F. Mexico:

Maya Cities, by Roman Piña Chan. 84 pages. A brief résumé of each of the principal Maya sites in Mexico, with illustrations of each.

Chichén Itzá, by Alberto Ruz. 48 pages, 1955.

Uxmal, by Alberto Ruz. 50 pages, 1959.

Palenque, by Alberto Ruz. 77 pages, 1960.

Tulúm, 47 pages, 1961.

All these pocket guides give excellent descriptions of their respective areas in clear, if a bit pedantic, English. Illustrations are poorly reproduced but adequate. All have good maps. Very well worth owning.

Maya
Cities

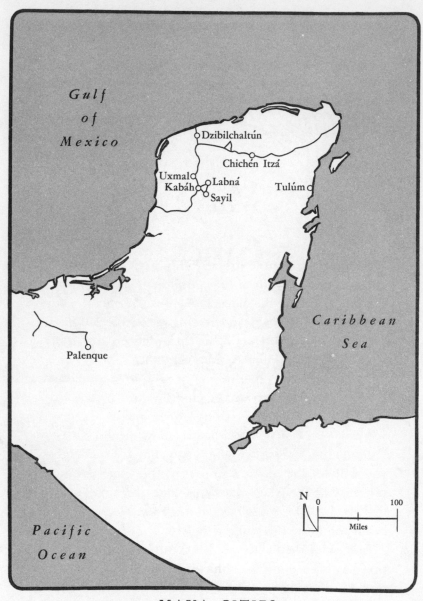

Gulf
of
Mexico

Dzibilchaltún

Chichén Itzá

Uxmal
Kabáh   Labná
            Sayil   Tulúm

Caribbean
Sea

Palenque

Pacific
Ocean

N   0   100
          Miles

MAYA CITIES

While there are, quite literally, hundreds of Maya cities and tens of thousands of Maya buildings spread through the jungle that is the Yucatán Peninsula, only a few of these are well known and readily accessible. Of these, Chichén Itzá and Uxmal are magnificent attractions, with excellent accommodations nearby.

Just as a viewer, standing on a hilltop overlooking a lovely valley, will first survey the panorama before using his binoculars for closer study of the details, so should you first visit Chichén Itzá before going on to Uxmal.

Both cities warrant close scrutiny, but at Chichén Itzá you will get the physical impact of the scope and magnificence of the Maya planning; and, therefore, at Uxmal you will be conscious, to a greater degree, of the beauty of the architectural details.

In both of these cities, too, a great amount of restoration has been done. Not that the cities have been "restored"—they are not Colonial Williamsburg! But a great deal of painstaking care and archaeological attention have been lavished upon these two cities, to assist you to the fullest in your appreciation and enjoyment of the Maya civilization.

You will never forget your first sight of the Castillo at Chichén, as it almost seems to spring out at you from above the jungle. Later impressions will only add to this, as you come to recognize the scope of the master plan that encompasses, not only the grand Castillo, but the squatter Temple of the Warriors, and the sweep of the Ball Court. And, as you become more sensitive to the wonders that are ever-present, you will feel the chill of a coldly staring Chac Mool, and the fierceness of tigers and eagles eternally tearing at human hearts.

At Uxmal, too, your first impression of the black bulk of the giant Pyramid of the Magician, towering over the once-thriving city, will be reinforced by the sheer beauty of the play of light and shade as sunshine and clouds sweep across the façade of the Palace of the Governor. Not only will you be conscious of the development of the buildings that compose the Nunnery Quadrangle there, but you will get a delightful warm feeling as you catch sight of the plump little owl on the North Building.

Your heart will be touched by the tinyness of the golden Temple of the Seven Dolls as it stands alone in the emptiness that is Dzibilchaltún. And you will come to realize, as you drive through the countryside, that these hillocks that you see everywhere are man-made, are themselves the relics of other temples and other palaces.

Palenque is, of course, totally different in setting.

Standing in the rain-forest jungle, a thousand feet up in the mountains of Chiapas, its pavilions contain some of the most exquisite sculpture ever brought forth by man.

Finally, you will come to realize that each Maya city is uniquely individual. When you have seen one, you have not seen them all, any more than seeing Chicago is the same as seeing San Francisco, or seeing New York is the same as seeing Boston. Each Maya city will thus become identifiable to you, for each has its own peculiarities of architecture and of sculptural detail. And you will love each one separately for what *it* has to offer.

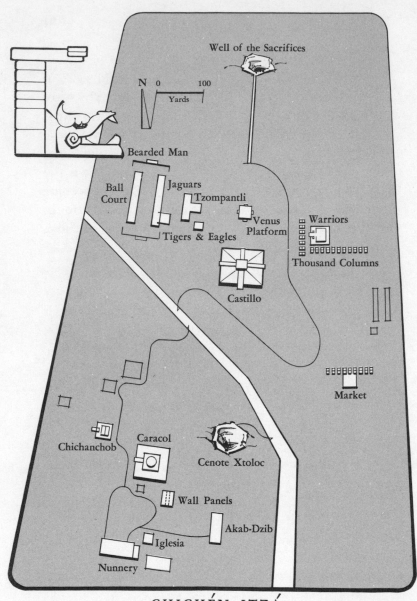

Well of the Sacrifices

N 0 100
Yards

Bearded Man

Ball Court
Jaguars
Tzompantli
Venus Platform
Warriors
Tigers & Eagles
Thousand Columns

Castillo

Market

Chichanchob
Caracol
Cenote Xtoloc

Wall Panels
Akab-Dzib
Iglesia
Nunnery

CHICHÉN ITZÁ

Chichén Itzá

As is the case with every city that man has built, Chichén Itzá has gone through periods of reconstruction and renewal. There were, you might say, three "foundings" of the city: its original construction; a wave of new building following the influx from the west of the Toltec conquerors of the Maya; and a period of decadence when different styles and themes were accented.

In general terms, for there is no presently unquestioned method of the exact determining of a date, the original buildings of Chichén Itzá were erected sometime subsequent to A.D. 432. About five hundred years later, placed by some archaeologists as around 964, the Toltec-Mexican wave reached Chichén, and a new rush of construction began. It was during this period that most of the buildings which are commonly associated with Chichén Itzá were built. Finally, only a couple of hundred years later, in 1185, a good deal of redesigning was done to older buildings, and savage, warlike themes dominated the sculptural works.

Water was a precious commodity, the heart of life in arid Yucatán, and the original buildings concentrated around the great natural well, Cenote Xtoloc. Of these, the Akab-Dzib (House of Obscure Writing) is probably the oldest. In the same neighborhood are the Nunnery and its Annex, the Iglesia, the House of the Deer, and Chichanchob (Red House). At some distance, in "Old Chichén," is the exquisite Temple of the Three Lintels, sometimes known as Paul Martin's Temple from the name of its restorer.

The "second founding" of Chichén occurred in the mid-tenth century when warlike invaders imposed their will upon the relatively peaceful Mayas. The invasion brought with it from Mexico the fierce worship of Kukulcán or Quetzalcóatl, the feathered serpent, and the cult of force and of death. Magnificent structures were erected during this period: the towering Castillo dominates the entire area; and the scarcely less magnificent Caracol is dedicated to the scientific study of the solar system. Also a part of this time were the Ball Court, whose games had a religious significance, and its accompanying Temple of the Jaguars. The Tzompantli, nearby, was crowned with row on row of skulls; and virgins, after being prepared on the Venus Platform, were flung into the Well of the Sacrifices. During this time the Temple of the Warriors, with its bulky serpent columns, was also built.

Finally decadence set in, as it once did at the legendary court of King Arthur and his Round Table, and form became more important than substance. Modifica-

tions were made to the buildings of "Old Chichén";
murals and carvings of war and warriors were added to
other buildings; and the warrior castes of the Tigers and
the Eagles were set apart and memorialized in stone.
And the Chac Mool, mindless, insensate, brooded over
all, caring not that human hearts, freshly torn from living bodies, were flung into his lap by frenzied worshipers.

You will find that the names of the buildings in Chichén Itzá may have little or nothing to do with their real
significance. The Nunnery is not a nunnery, nor the
Castillo a castle. They are still known by the names the
Spaniards gave them—likened to Old World structures
—when they first glimpsed them over four hundred
years ago.

Just as the Maya cities were, almost without exception, not cities in our sense but ceremonial centers, so
too is the Castillo not the residence of a king but a
temple to Kukulcán.

Your first impulse will be to climb it as soon as you
enter the archaeological zone, but you will do better if
you just wander around, getting the feel of the place,
and noting where various structures are and what they
look like.

As you enter the main gate after buying your 2-peso
ticket and signing the guest book, you come out on a
huge, closely mown grassy field, or lawn. (Before exploring, find out what hours the interior temples of the Castillo, the Jaguars, and the Warriors are open.) On your

right rises the Castillo, and peering over its far corner is the smaller pyramid of the Temple of the Warriors, topped with columns silhouetted against the blue sky. Directly ahead is a grove of trees, among which you will later distinguish the Tzompantli, and the Platform of the Tigers and Eagles. The Well of the Sacrifices is out of sight, a couple of hundred yards down a jungle road past the Venus Platform. A bit to the left as you stand at the entrance are the high, heavy walls of the Ball Court, the nearer corner being topped by the Temple of the Jaguars—its upper shrine facing toward the court, the lower one facing the Castillo.

The Central Area of Chichén Itzá is separated from the northern one described above not only by the main highway that runs between Mérida and Valladolid but also by a thick strip of jungle through which a path leads from a stile at the roadside, a hundred yards or so, to the Ossuary, or Grave of the High Priest. This mound, on the right of the path, is topped with the remains of a temple. Back a few feet in the jungle a bit further on is another ruin, the House of the Corn Grinders. You then break into the open before the well-preserved Chichan-chob, on a steep-sided mound of its own. Passing between low rises that cannot be distinguished as a ball court, except for some carved stones, you find the majestic circular Caracol on your left, on a big platform. Beyond it, and down hill a bit is the Temple of the Wall Panels. The Nunnery itself is a massive pile, but its Annex, to its east, is light and lovely. The Iglesia almost touches the Annex, at a slight angle. A path running

back a few yards into the jungle will lead you to the
Akab-Dzib. The Cenote Xtoloc is not accessible from
this side, but is reached by a trail into the woods a short
distance up from the Hotel Mayaland.

To get to "Old Chichén"—after getting yourself well
sprayed—go into the grounds of the Hacienda Chichén,
following an old narrow-gauge railroad track, leaving
the Church of San Isidro on your left. About a mile in,
this cow path through the jungle splits, and you go down
the right-hand one. A bit further along, through what
remains of an arch (not much), you'll come upon a cluster of structures. The long, low building facing you is
the Temple of the Phalli, and on your left on a high
mound, the Date Group with its high Atlantean columns surmounted by a carved lintel. In a semicircle
back of and partly surrounding the Phalli are the ruins of
the Temple of the Naked Children, the Owl, and the
Caryatids. Hidden in the edge of the jungle between the
arch and the Naked Children is a stone iguana and a
decayed Chac Mool. Keep going in this direction about
another half mile, and you'll come to the beautifully restored Temple of the Three Lintels, passing on the way
the ruins of the Temple of the Lintel and the Temple of
the Four Lintels. You may also notice, about halfway
along, in the jungle on your right, a *chultun,* or well for
water storage. Be careful to look where you're going in
order not to fall into it! You will also cross, and partially
follow, the remains of an old *sacbe,* or ceremonial road,
looking like a lengthy pile of stones, leveling off the surface of the ground.

Before you came to the Date Group area, if you had taken the left fork you would have come to the Temple of the Hieroglyphic Jambs; and if you had taken an invisible trail to the right you would have come to the Bird Cornice and its contiguous buildings . . . and really have gotten *garrapatas* all over you—which wouldn't have been worth the trouble.

THE BUILDINGS OF CHICHÉN ITZÁ

North Area

THE CASTILLO   As cannot be too often repeated, the Castillo or the Temple of Kukulcán dominates one's thinking of Chichén Itzá. This gray mass, 100 feet high and 180 feet square at its base, rises steeply from the short-cropped grass and seems to be constantly at your side wherever you go in this area.

While believed by Bishop Landa to be dedicated to Kukulcán (the plumed serpent god)—from *kuk,* quetzal bird; *ul,* feathers; *can,* serpent—it is actually more probably a temple to the Sun. There are 91 steps on each of the 4 sides—a total of 364 in all—which, plus the upper platform, adds up to 365, the number of days in the year. And there are 9 terraces on each side, each split by the central stairway. These 18 correspond with the number of months in the Mayan calendar. Finally, each side of the pyramid has 52 panels contained in its terraces which is the same as the number of years in the Mayan calendric cycle.

The principal face of the structure is the north, where the balustrade ends at ground level in two gigantic open-mouthed serpent heads. You will ascend, however, by the west stairway, where a chain has been placed for your convenience and safety. Going up is no problem: simply keep your weight forward and your hands loosely on the chain and walk up, leaning in. Getting started coming down is initially terrifying, since you look over the edge of the steep drop at the ground so far below. But, once you've started and gotten the hang of it, you'll end by going up and down without considering it. To come down: sit, and work your way over to the edge by the chain. (See why blue jeans are recommended?) Turn sidewise, whether to left or right, whichever is more comfortable, although facing inboard is suggested, and put your leg over the edge, feeling for the first step and holding onto the chain. Then go down hand over hand, keeping your body pitched inward at almost the angle of the stairway. Be sure one foot is firmly on a lower step before you move the other. Pretty soon you'll be looking out or down, and surveying the sights.

As you climbed the stairs, you undoubtedly wondered why the old-time Maya ever made them so steep. For not only is the height of each riser much greater than what we are accustomed to, but this is accentuated by the narrowness of the step itself. That a people as short as the Maya should have done this seems inconceivable.

Yet it was done deliberately; and probably because the Maya were a little people, not in spite of that fact. Imagine a procession of priests ascending the stairway of

the tall pyramid to the sanctuary of the Temple of Kukulcán—plumed headdresses sweeping almost to their
feet, bells tied to their ankles, some with gourd rattles,
some with flutes or whistles or drums. The parade across
the great courtyard must have been an awe-inspiring
sight. As it approaches the foot of the stairway, the four-
abreast column splits into single file.

The very narrowness of the treads compels the line of
priests to climb the steps diagonally, to move upward
across the stairway. When the line reaches the balustrade, it reverses itself, and recrosses the steps while still
moving upward, shifting its direction each time it
reaches the boundary of the broad stairway.

Each riser is high, especially in relation to the stature
of the priests. Therefore, each stepping movement of
each individual is accentuated, and the line appears to
undulate as it weaves upward. The feathered serpent of
Kukulcán comes alive!

But while you're on top of the Castillo there's a lot to
see. First of all, after you've recovered your breath look
around! For here is Chichén Itzá at your feet. Tiny people walking on the grass below, the bulk of the Ball
Court, the Temple of the Warriors, suprisingly small
from your lofty perch, the round of the Caracol, and the
mass of the Nunnery, even your own *casita* at the Mayaland—and all surrounded by unending miles of gray-
green jungle, stretching into the horizon. The works of
man are mighty, but the works of God are infinite. No
wonder man has always erected temples to His worship,

no matter what His guise may have been in other cultures.

The north portico of the temple centers upon two serpent columns, similar to but not in as good shape as the ones on the Temple of the Warriors. The cornice and frieze are plain, except for a mask of Chac, the Rain God, over the doorway. But what you are really up here for is the view, for there is little of the temple that demands your attention.

At the base of the north stairway you will see a small door which is kept locked except for two hours a day: once in the morning and once in the afternoon. (From your earlier inquiry at the gatehouse, you will have learned the times at which this inner temple—and the others mentioned—are open.)

Entering here, you will climb a narrow, brightly lighted stairway that is neither so steep nor so high as that on the exterior and come upon an interior temple, containing "the most outstanding archaeological object ever discovered in the New World."

The Mayas had the custom, throughout the entire area of their cities, of building one temple upon another. Apparently the older temple outlived its usefulness, or its power, or, perhaps it just wasn't big enough to suit the new generation. At any rate, the Mayas would just cover up the old with another pyramidal layer to erect a higher, bigger temple.

In this interior Temple of Kukulcán, unearthed almost by accident, are two superbly beautiful objects.

The one considered an outstanding find is the Red Jaguar Throne. The stone animal is painted a brilliant red, with inset jade eyes and spots. Perfectly preserved, its fierce mouth snarls at the beholder. Its back is inset with a flat plate upon which incense was burned and which represents the sun.

Guarding the Red Jaguar from an antechamber is a Chac Mool, with incrustations of shell for the eyes, teeth, and fingernails. As you know, a number of these staring, mindless, reclining figures are found in the area of Chichén Itzá, evidence of the cult of human sacrifice that existed here under the Toltecs.

If your time is limited, there are certain "musts" aside from the Castillo: the Ball Court and the Temple of the Warriors nearby, and the Caracol and the Iglesia across the road. But don't hurry. See the various structures in easy sequence, so that, later, you may come back for another look at your favorites.

THE TEMPLE OF THE WARRIORS   Your next climb, and an easy one it is, is up the broad steps of the Temple of the Warriors. As you approach this building, you will pass through a colonnade of square columns, each elaborately carved with the figure of a plumed warrior. Originally this area had a flat roof, probably of plastered wattle, and was used as a council hall or as an anteroom to the upper temple.

As you ascend the steps you come out on a broad platform. Immediately facing you is the figure of a Chac Mool. Look well, for upon the lap of this prone stone figure with its expressionless face were flung hearts freshly torn from human bodies as sacrifices were offered to the serpent god, Kukulcán.

Flanking the top of the stairway are two dwarf-like figures called Standard Bearers. Holes in their hands made them capable of holding staffs from which plumes waved. Framing the Chac Mool are two gigantic serpent columns. The base is the head, with wide open jaws protruding; the column is the body; and, balanced on the top, the capital rises once again to form the tail. Here it seems probable that a flat, beamed roof was used rather than the corbeled vault, which you will see so much of later.

The exterior frieze is decorated with triple masks of Chac, the Rain God. The curled nose, with raindrops coursing down it, is the most prominent feature; but you can imagine clearly the open mouth, the squared eyes, and the ear lobes with their plugs.

Between the masks are very handsome serpent-bird panels with great plumes richly carved in relief. A serpent's head, whose wide-stretched jaws hold a human head, protrudes from the center of each panel. You will enjoy walking around the broad platform, examining the frieze and looking out at the countryside.

Against the rear wall of the inner temple behind the Chac Mool is a broad altar, held aloft by Atlantean columns. This type of column, also found in "Old Chichén," depicts a person with upraised hands supporting, in this case, the altar table. (The columns, of course, take their name from the Greek god who bore the world upon his shoulders.) Interestingly enough, measurements indicate that this altar was originally placed in what is now the interior temple.

While you are on the platform, if it is the proper hour, you will do well to descend the few steps into this interior temple. Its colums and walls were once painted with murals depicting life in a Mayan village, but these are no longer visible, and only traces of their brilliant color remain. What makes your descent worthwhile, however, is another Chac Mool, this one with a peculiar frog headdress.

Those of you who have arrived in Yucatán from Mexico City will have felt a familiarity with the Temple of the Warriors, for it represents the same Toltec civilization you have seen at Tula, sixty miles north of the capital. There, too, are colonnades of carven warriors and representations of the plumed serpent. In Tula the god was called Quetzalcóatl, but he was still the same person, a man who became divine and was perhaps reincarnated here.

When you come down from the outer temple, notice the three decorated cornices that mark each terrace. For one thing, they extend beneath the stairway, indicating that the terraces were added at a later date. Too, they are oddly repetitious, running to units of four figures: a jaguar, an eagle, a warrior and—is it a monkey?—something the Carnegie Institution archaeologists christened a "Woolly."

THE MARKET AND THE GROUP OF THE THOUSAND COL-
UMNS South, across the colonnaded plaza, is an area
that has been called the Market, again for convenience'
sake rather than in the belief that it actually served this
purpose, since its carvings are also of a warlike nature.
It is more rubble than ruins, and you may wish to omit
it in favor of spending additional time elsewhere.

But it is interesting to speculate on this whole mass of
the Thousand Columns, for it virtually surrounds an
area of about six acres. Immediately in front of the
Temple of the Warriors, the pillars are square and are
all carved; but around the rest of the group only one row
of carved square columns makes a front for plain, drum-
like ones. Probably the entire space of the collonnade
was covered with a light thatch; it could have corre-
sponded with medieval cloisters, where priests or nobles
could walk in the cool shade and meditate.

In this area also are two small ball courts, both in poor
condition, and the remains of a steam bath, which was
used for purificational rites. It consists of a portico, or
waiting room; a low-roofed steam room with an adjoin-
ing walk where red-hot rocks were placed and water
flung upon them; and an oven in the rear to heat stones.
There is a canal for drainage and windows for ventilation.

VENUS PLATFORM AND WELL OF THE SACRIFICES
Moving counterclockwise from the Temple of the
Warriors you come to the Venus Platform. This time
there is a reason for the name. Not that it is connected

with the Venus of Roman mythology, whom we think of in connection with beautiful women; but rather it is named after the planet Venus, the brightest of the heavenly bodies after the sun and moon. This is known from the sign of the planet, a carving that is repeated around the frieze.

This small square platform, about 6 feet high, may be reached by 4 wide stairways, each surmounted by a serpent's head. Legend has it, and it is no more than legend, that lovely virgins were prepared here prior to being flung into the Sacred Cenote.

Actually, when it was being restored, a Chac Mool was found in its interior—not in a temple, just buried amid the rubble. In the recessed panels of the wall are delicately carved representations of Kukulcán.

About a quarter mile down a pleasant road through the jungle is the Well of the Sacrifices, an artificially rounded *cenote* almost 200 feet across, and about 60 feet from the surface to water level.

A *cenote*, you will recall, represents the only source of water for much of the year in arid Yucatán, yet this one was apparently used exclusively for ritualistic purposes. As a consequence, divers have been sent down by archaeologists to plumb the depths (about 40 feet plus 10 feet of mud) and to bring up many beautiful objects of gold and precious stones. Curiously, most are of a relatively late date (thirteenth to sixteenth centuries) and from distant parts of Central or even South America, rather than being of local origin and of a period contemporaneous with the flourishing of Chichén Itzá.

By the way, you can drive your car to the Sacred Cenote, or Well of the Sacrifices. If you've already parked your car within the gates and paid your small fee (as you probably have) simply follow the road past the Castillo in front of the Temple of the Warriors, which leads you to the Well. And this might make it easy for you to see the Market and the two small ball courts—just pull your car to the side of the road and walk in.

PLATFORM OF THE TIGERS AND EAGLES AND TZOMPANTLI

Continuing counterclockwise from the Venus Platform, you come to two others. The first, that of the Tigers and Eagles, is virtually indistinguishable in appearance from the Venus. Only the sculptural designs differ. Here we find tigers and eagles holding human hearts in their claws. This area, then, is clearly Toltec, and was dedicated to the military orders bearing these names, whose prisoners were sacrificed to the god Kukulcán, evidenced by the feathered serpent whose image appears on the balustrades.

The Tzompantli is still another platform, but this time larger and tau-shaped. It gets its name from the Aztec word for Wall of Skulls, and, indeed, its entire frieze is a repetition of this theme, plus a few panels devoted to the Tigers and Eagles who furnished the victims.

TEMPLE OF THE JAGUARS   Just before you enter the precincts of the Ball Court, you come upon a ground-level structure, the lower temple. In its central doorway is a stone statue of a jaguar; and its walls and pillars are beautifully carved with figures of priests and nobles in full panoply. These are truly wonderful to see, and deserve careful scrutiny, for, once you begin to get the idea of what is shown, you see more and more, and become increasingly interested, for the four superposed horizontal bands tell a story. A feathered serpent rises through

Chichén Itzá, Platform of the Tigers and Eagles: Jaguar contemplating human heart

two adjacent bands, attacking a warlike tribe above, while, near its tail, priests hold ears of corn, and come in a boat to worship him. On the left column there is a beautifully carved old man, probably representing It-zamná, the son of the principal god.

Around the corner you climb short, but steep, stairs to the upper temple, located on the southeast corner of the Ball Court. The temple gets its name from the band of marching jaguars on its frieze, a beautifully executed decorative effect. With its giant serpent columns supporting the doorway, this temple, too, is typically Toltec.

The interior of this upper temple is the third place where you will have to time your visit to coincide with the hours of admission. Contained here is what was once described as "the greatest gem of aboriginal art on the whole continent of America that still survives, though badly mutilated." Sadly, the key words are the last two, for little is left of a once-gorgeous polychrome relief that depicted tales of battle, worship, and daily life in Yuca-tán a thousand years ago. Colors are faded, and so much is defaced that its wonder is truly gone.

BALL COURT AND TEMPLE OF THE BEARDED MAN

While you are on the upper level of the Temple of the Jaguars you will want to walk along the top of the inner side of the Ball Court in order to get a close look at the carved stone ring that protrudes from the wall, not hori-zontally like a basketball hoop, but vertically. It is finely carved to represent intertwined serpents attacking each other, and has survived the centuries well, although it could do with a bit of cleaning to remove the lichen that obscure its details.

It is believed that the game was played with a rubber ball about the size of our softball, between teams of seven players, on an area about the size and shape of a football field. As in soccer, use of the hands was not permitted—but neither could feet be used, so a player had to be pretty agile with his elbows, knees, and hips! Points could be scored in various ways, as in court tennis, but the game could be brought to a summary conclusion if the ball was hit through one of the stone rings. Indeed if this was accomplished in the "World Series," the captain of the losing team was beheaded. For the game was a religious ceremony fully as much as a sport, and the blood sacrifice thus became part of a fertility rite.

This fact is shown clearly on two panels of bas-relief in the center of the Ball Court at ground level. Cutting through the mass of detail (for you will already have noticed that Maya artists seemed impelled to cover every inch of stone), you will make out a central disk representing a death's-head. On its right is a decapitated kneeling figure, the losing captain, from whose neck issue serpents (life). Facing him are the members of the winning team, its captain carrying a knife in one hand and the upside-down, severed head of his opponent in the other. Further panels tell similar stories, depicting various phases of the game.

At the north end of the Ball Court is the Temple of the Bearded Man, so-called from the hirsute adornment of one of its principal sculptures. It is interesting to climb up into it, for people speaking in normal tones in its back corners can readily be heard throughout the Ball Court and at the ruins of a corresponding temple more than a hundred yards away.

Central Area

GRAVE OF THE HIGH PRIEST (OSSUARY)   After you leave the North Area, you will go about a hundred yards down the main road toward your hotel. Here, on the right, is a concrete stile leading to a broad path. After following this for a short distance, you will see on your right a high, ruined mound, surmounted by two huge serpent-heads and a lonely standing pillar. The Ossuary, or Grave of the High Priest, stands above an underground cave connected by a shaft with the top, and it contains bones and offerings dating from the Toltec period. It is picturesque to look at, but does not require a closer view.

A short distance beyond, also on the right, a trail leads in to the House of the Corn Grinders, another ruin and also not worth extra efforts, as there are only a couple of overthrown Atlantean columns left. The same is true of the House of the Deer, standing on the edge of a clearing beyond and not even connected with your roadway.

CHICHANCHOB   This temple, on a high mound overlooking a narrow and decayed small ball court, is well worth your trouble. It has many names: Chichanchob

(Maya for "small holes," referring to its pierced roof comb); Casa Colorada or Red House (derived from a red strip that was once on the wall of the portico). It is among the early buildings of Chichén Itzá, definitely Classic Maya in its architecture.

You will notice that the exterior of the building itself is completely plain; that all decoration is confined to its flying façade (like the "false front" of buildings of our old West) and to the roof comb (a similar wall, but centrally located, running the width of the building, and used not only for the decoration that it supports, but as a weight to reinforce the balance of the corbeled vault). This flying façade is decorated with the "Greek key" design (an angled spiral) and with masks of Chac over each doorway.

Another point that distinguishes this building is that it is built on a platform whose corners are not square but rounded. The Mirador at Labná, and the Advino at Uxmal are similarly constructed. There is also a long strip of stone hieroglyphs on the cornice of the front room worth noting.

THE CARACOL   You are now out in a large cleared area, with the Nunnery facing you, and on your left the circular, high Observatory, or Caracol, "snail" in English. Its name refers to the spiral stairway in its interior, but the building was designed as an astronomical observatory. Research has determined that sightings taken through various apertures in the outer and inner walls of the tower mark exactly such occasions as sunrise or

sunset on the longest or shortest days of the year, as well
as certain phases of the moon, and data on the planet
Venus.

It was from such calculations as these, kept over hundreds of years, that the Maya priests derived much of
their power. For they were thus enabled to predict with
exactitude many natural phenomena: not only such
major ones as eclipses, but important regular occur-
rences like the coming of the rainy or the dry seasons,
which set the sowing and harvesting of the crops. Indeed, some authorities believe that sudden flood or
drought, unpredicted by the priests, actually caused the
downfall of the Maya civilization by leading to a rebel-
lion of the peasantry in which priests and nobles were
exterminated.

When you climb to the rectangular platform upon
which the Caracol is based, you can clearly see the various super-positions that were made before the building
reached its final form. Started in A.D. 900, the original
building consisted of a great platform upon which a circular tower was erected: the tower consisted of a solid
lower body and an intermediate body with two circular
galleries around which a spiral stair ascended to the ob-
servation chamber (you must now use a ladder to reach
this chamber). You can distinguish various additions,
until the final form, with its rectangular parapet, was
achieved. The incense pots that rim this parapet are
shaped like human heads.

The balustrades of the main stairway are two intertwined serpents; and in the center of this stair is an al-

cove for a stele or *picote*. This is an immensely rewarding building, not only for its beauty (round Maya buildings are very rare), but for its contribution to the development of a highly sophisticated calendar. Indeed, it
seems quite possible that Bishop Landa's recognition of
the Mayas' calculation of the length of the year led to
the adoption of the Gregorian calendar under which we
live today.

TEMPLE OF THE WALL PANELS As you come down
from the Caracol, keeping to the left side of the field,
you will pass by the ruins of a small temple—and a sweat
house, unroofed, with a circular tub set into the ground
with steps leading to it.

Further along on this east side is the Temple of the
Wall Panels, which contains a couple of items of real interest. First of these is, of course, the sculptured areas on
its north and south exteriors that gave the temple its
name. Each panel shows three rows of people with warriors, serpents, and birds. It is probably Toltec, and refers to their military orders. The south panel is the
clearer of the two.

Actually the construction of the temple is rather peculiar. The main temple is on a high mound, and to
reach it today you have to clamber around the south
side, where the panel is located on its base. But it is evident that at one time proper access was gained over the
roof of the lower forward temple, for here are stairs and
a vaulted passage.

You will find that this short passage offers you an op-

Pan Am

Chichén Itzá: The Castillo from the Platform of Venus

Chichén Itzá: A corner of the Ball Court with the Temple
of the Jaguars; in the distance, Warriors and the Castillo

Mexican National Tourist Council

Mexican Gov't Tourism Dep

Chichén Itzá: Serpent Columns of the Temple of the Warriors

Chichén Itzá: The Caracol

Chichén Itzá: The Lower Jaguar Temple and the Platform
of the Tigers and Eagles

Chichén Itzá: The Ball Court

Henry F. Godfrey

Old Chichén": The Temple of the Three Lintels

Dzibilchaltún: The Temple of the Seven Dolls

Mexican Gov't Tourism Dept.

Uxmal: Façade of the Palace of the Governor; in the distance, the Advino

Uxmal: The House of the Turtles

Uxmal: The Palace of the Governor

Uxmal: Two-headed Jaguar Throne on the terrace in front of the Palace of the Governor

Uxmal: The Nunnery Quadrangle—North Building and the Temple of Venus

xmal: The Nunnery Quadrangle—detail of frieze of West uilding

xmal: The Nunnery Quadrangle—detail of frieze of East uilding

Uxmal: West face of the Advino, showing Chenes Temple

ayil: The Palace—Alligator and Diving God on frieze over
oorway

ayil: The Palace—Chac mask over doorway

Henry F. Godfre

Labná: Corner of the Palace, showing sculpture of head in serpent's jaws; in the distance, the Mirador. The tree at right foreground is Stephens' "noble ramon"

Labná: The Arch

Tulúm: The Castillo and the Temple of the Diving God

Kabáh: Chac masks from the façade of the Codz-Pop

Palenque: The Palace, the Temple of the Sun, and the Temple of the Inscriptions

Palenque: The Temple of the Inscriptions

Palenque: The Temple of the Cross—relief showing Old
Man smoking

portunity to examine at close range the method of construction of a corbeled vault. The principle of the keystone arch was unknown to the Maya, a fact that severely limited the width of their rooms. In its place they developed the corbeled arch. In this, stones are lapped inward from the top of the wall until they get close enough for a flat capstone to be placed across the opening. As a result, Maya rooms are high and narrow. Here you can see clearly the method of workmanship. On the wall a "shoe-shaped" stone is placed, with rubble weighting down its outer side. On top of this, another similar stone, and so on (in this case, just these two) until the capstone can be laid transversely across the opening to form the ceiling. Notice, too, how carefully the stones are finished, so that walls and corbeling meet at neat, precise angles—and remember that the Maya had no metal tools.

AKAB-DZIB   While you are on this east side, follow the path to the left for a short distance to view what is probably the oldest building in all Chichén Itzá, the House of Obscure Writing. Long and low, with unadorned walls, simple cornices and moldings, it is a lovely structure, typically Classic Maya in decoration.

As you approach it from the south, you will be able to find the "obscure writings." Stand in the south doorway and look up—directly over your head. There on the soffit (underside of the lintel) is carved the sitting figure of a priest, on a throne before an incensory. Hieroglyphs, still undeciphered, ring the figure and the lintel. Note especially the "tin woodsman-like" nose of the figure, so utterly unlike the Maya profile and which has been found nowhere else except at Kabáh, a circumstance that makes the "obscure writings" even more inexplicable. You will find other soffits that have been carved with hieroglyphs, but none with a scene.

Now go down the west side and enter the second room. There you will see the prints of the red hand. Some say that such prints, which you will find elsewhere, are a possible symbol of Zamná, the god of the heavenly hand. What seems more probable is that such prints, which are quite literally the prints of a human hand and not painted or stenciled, represent an attempt on the part of the humble laborer to identify perpetually his part in the construction of these magnificent religious buildings. They were never intended to be seen, for they appear only where the outer layer of smooth, often decorated stucco has fallen away. It is touching to note that, fifteen hundred years ago, some man so lovingly worshiped his god that he made an individual part of himself (for are not today fingerprints recognized as wholly distinctive?) a part of a beauty beyond his imaginings.

THE NUNNERY, THE ANNEX, AND THE IGLESIA You now return to a group of three buildings, with some quite ruined adjacent structures. The Nunnery itself is a rather amorphous mass of fallen masonry, but the east façade of the Annex and the Iglesia are exquisite. You will remember, by the way, that the Nunnery was the name given by the Spaniards, whom it reminded—by its many rooms—of the convents of their own country; you must not try to imagine vestal virgins and savage rites connected with it!

First, notice the contrast between the architectural styles of the Annex and the Iglesia. The former is in what is called the Chenes (well) style, with both frieze and façade (in other words, the whole face of the building) decorated. The latter is in Puuc (hill) style, with a plain façade and a decorated frieze. Yet both are Classic Maya in origin, and are approximately contemporaneous.

The entire eastern side of the Annex, from ground to roof, is composed of masks of Chac, the long-nosed God of Rain. Around the cornices runs an undulating line representing a serpent, and over the doorway, within a sunburst halo, sits a richly clad figure. Notice the fangs above the door, which give the entire area the appearance of the mouth of a mask.

The Iglesia is a little gem. Set just off the corner of the Annex, it is almost a cube. Its lower wall is undecorated, made of rather rough stone that was originally covered with smooth stucco. Above this are two cornices, separated by a narrow band of "Greek keys." Above this is a wide frieze, three sides of which have huge masks of Chac separated by the keys. On the west side, where the doorway is, the fierce masks are separated by twin panels bearing figures of the four Bacabs (the gods whose duty it was to hold up the sky): an armadillo, a snail, a turtle, and a crab (viewing from north to south). Above this are two still narrower cornices, split by another serpentine motif; and finally a magnificent roof comb, decorated on the west by masks of Chac, and on the rear by a stone latticework design.

THE CENOTE XTOLOC   While not now directly accessible from the Central Area, the Cenote Xtoloc was the principal well around which the life of early Chichén Itzá revolved. It is now easily reached by a path on the left of the main road, between the hotels and Chichén Itzá. It was not a sacred place (although there are the negligible remains of a small temple near its edge), but the water source for the city. A ramp leads down to the water, and, in its natural jungle setting, it is highly picturesque. You can picture the explorer John Lloyd Stephens and his companions bathing here, relaxing from the heat of midday, leaving strict orders that they were not to be disturbed by the curious stares of the natives, who came all the way from Pisté to gape at these strange white men more than a century ago.

"Old Chichén"

One of the principal reasons for walking to "Old Chichén" is that so very few people do. As a result—with one exception—the buildings are in ruder state, and you are rewarded by feeling like an explorer. The path is wide and pleasantly shaded, and, once you are well sprayed, you need not worry about the *garrapatas*. Nor will any animal wilder than a wandering cow or pony, or the fierce-looking but harmless dragon that is an iguana, disturb your leisure.

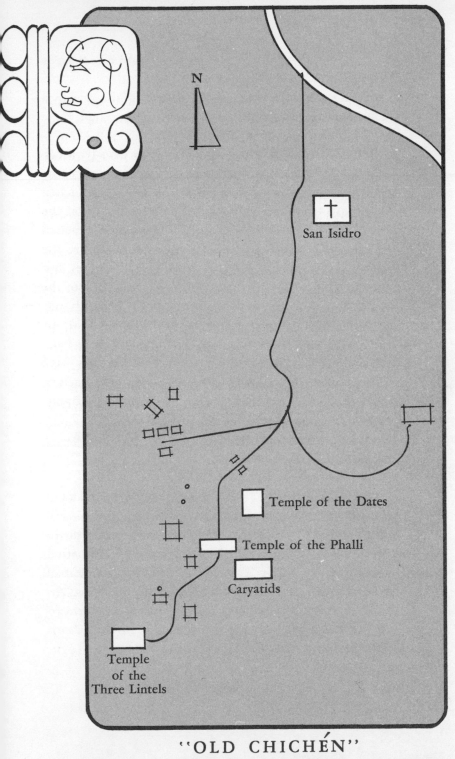

N

San Isidro

Temple of the Dates

Temple of the Phalli

Caryatids

Temple
of the
Three Lintels

"OLD CHICHÉN"

But you will really feel that you have gone back into an earlier time, away from the voices and bustle of the other areas. There is a caretaker and his family at the Date Group (a general term for a number of structures) who will be more than happy to show you around, and describe the place to you. (A tip of 3 or 4 pesos above the admission fee on your departure will be thoughtful of you.)

Follow the main road along a narrow-gauge railroad (once used to transport henequen) through the gates of the Hacienda Chichén. The Church of San Isidro on your left is typical of the small churches that are found on all *haciendas* throughout Central America, simple stucco, with the bells still hanging in its belfry to call the Indian families to Mass.

Some Indian houses will be on your right as you walk over a slight rise and down a wide path under towering trees. After about three quarters of a mile, you will come to a split, where you will take the right fork that leads shortly to the Date Group.

THE DATE GROUP   Just as you enter this cleared area, you will pass between two stone piles which once probably constituted an arch, but now are nondescript mounds. On your left, on a high mound silhouetted against the sky, is the TEMPLE OF THE DATES, so-called because of the lintel carried on the heads of the two Atlantean columns on which hieroglyphs are carved bearing the date A.D. 879. Since the date is of the Classic Maya period and Atlanteans did not come into vogue until the arrival of the Toltecs, it is obvious that the lintel was removed from an earlier building.

Directly ahead of you is the low mound of the TEMPLE OF THE PHALLI. These objects jut from the center of the walls, which are otherwise bare. It should be recognized that it was not the original intent that such devices be erotic, but, rather that they are a symbol of fertility in a religious rite. And while the temple itself is of lovely Classic Maya simplicity, the phalli only became a part of Maya culture with the Toltecs.

Like the Temple of the Phalli, all other structures in "Old Chichén" are built at ground level, except for the Temple of the Dates. And, while many are pretty much decayed, nonetheless this very wildness is part of the charm of the area.

The TEMPLE OF THE NAKED CHILDREN (sometimes called Temple of the Little Heads) consists now of overthrown columns on which are sculptured unclothed youths. The OWLS is named from the birds that are represented on its columns. The CARYATIDS has Atlantean columns of huge proportions.

On the edge of the nearby jungle is an old Chac Mool. Despite his general decay, he remains an impressive figure, lying half-hidden amid the brush. Near him is a large stone sculpture of an iguana, as gray and ugly as his prototype, but a thousand times larger.

Running south from this area is a further path that later crosses what is called a *sacbe,* a sacred road. Such roads ran straight and level between cities, built up where needed, and originally surfaced with smooth cement. As the Mayas did not have the wheel, these roads were used for communication, and for the transportation of priests and nobles in litters on the shoulders of their servants.

Off to the right of your path, a few yards into the brush, is a *chultun,* a cistern, which the ancient Maya used for the collection and storage of water. Even today, you can see the stone channels that they built to direct rainwater into this cement-lined pit.

Here also are the ruins of two more structures, the TEMPLE OF THE LINTEL and the TEMPLE OF THE FOUR LINTELS, each so-called from the number of sculptured door-headings that remain. Some of their glyphs are very clear and interesting to inspect more closely.

Even if the generally ruined appearance of what you have thus far seen in the area has failed to interest you, you will be struck by the beauty of the finely restored TEMPLE OF THE THREE LINTELS, or Paul Martin's Temple as it is sometimes called.

Each of its three doors has its beautifully sculptured lintel still in place. As in the case of the earlier ones you have seen, these too are date glyphs, but have not yet been deciphered.

The building itself is in almost perfect condition, and represents an almost pure example of the Classic Maya period, with its simple lines and restrained decoration.

It is set upon a lattice base, from which rises an unadorned façade. Above this is a cornice with a narrow band of angled lines. The frieze is simple and beautiful, latticed panels alternating with groups of thin columns.

The corners, both of the pediment and the frieze, are masks of Chac.

All your efforts in walking the two miles to this temple have been more than repaid.

The Cave of Balancanche

A few miles down the road toward Valladolid, then off on a short spur of a dirt road to the left, is the wondrous Cave of Balancanche. Accidentally discovered only in 1959, it provides one of the most interesting insights into Maya religious customs.

The cave is only open at certain hours, and one may only enter when accompanied by a local guide. You enter through a grove of trees into a natural cavern formed by a watercourse. The cave is not cold, or damp, nor does it induce a feeling of claustrophobia. It is well-lit, the path is clear and smooth, and, except for a distance of about fifteen feet, it is very spacious.

What you will see is unique. Here are Maya artifacts, richly decorated urns and simple *metates* (corn-grinding stones), exactly as they were placed there by reverent hands a thousand years ago. Only the dust of ages has been blown from them; otherwise they stand as they stood then.

The holy of holies is a giant "room" where a huge stalactite and stalagmite have joined together to form what appears to be a tremendous ceiba tree, its bronze-colored trunk six feet in diameter. Above it, on the spreading roof, tiny stalactites look like the leaves on its

branches. Here, according to the ancient priests, earth
and heaven were joined, and here the gods were worshiped.

Marking the boundaries of the entrance path are two
censers, and you halt here, preparing your mind for
what you are about to see.

Around the base of the altar-tree are placed urns, so
decorated as to resemble masks of Chac, the Rain God.
They are hourglass-shaped, about a foot or more tall,
and made of brown earthenware. Others are dedicated
to Chac's Toltec counterpart, the mustachioed god
Tláloc. And there are bowls, or tall jars, that once may
have held offerings of food or drink. The countless *metates* are paired with *manos,* the stone rollers for crushing
the kernels by hand. There is a stone heart, representing
a sacrificial offering. And a nearby column has been cut
in two, to provide a crude jaguar throne. On the trunk
of the tree-altar are upside-down handprints, made there
by priests as they prayed—a thousand years ago.

Descending past this until you are about a quarter
mile in and about sixty feet down, you come upon the
still waters of a lake where blind fish swim.

In its center, on a pile of stones forming a crude altar,
is a single Tláloc urn, alone, beseeching its god . . .
century after century.

Dzibilchaltún

The road from Mérida to Progreso runs straight north. About twelve miles from the city, a newly paved spur leads a few miles to the right to what may well prove to be the ancient Mayas' largest and oldest city. Legend tells us of the huge city of T'ho, and has long coupled its name with that of Mérida itself. But, as more intensive exploratory work is conducted at Dzibilchaltún, it becomes apparent that here was, indeed, a gigantic city, one covering twenty square miles, and with a continuous record of occupation from 2000 B.C. until the Spanish conquest. It has also been determined that Dzibilchaltún was a real city, not just a ceremonial center, where perhaps a quarter million people lived.

The name means "Where There Is Writing on Flat Stones," and there are several excellent examples of stelae on exhibit in the good little museum near the entrance gate. These stelae are monument-sized slabs, about 6 or 8 feet tall, with a 2½-foot face on which is sculptured a priestly figure and some hieroglyphs. They

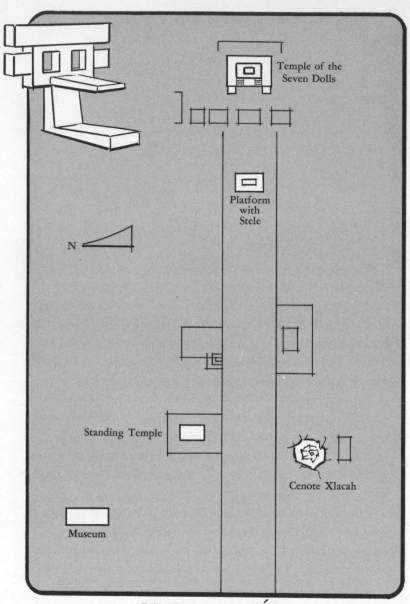

Temple of the
Seven Dolls

Platform
with
Stele

N

Standing Temple

Cenote Xlacah

Museum

DZIBILCHALTÚN

are usually believed to commemorate the closing of a *katun,* a period of time roughly corresponding to twenty years.

The Dzibilchaltún that you see adjoins a central *sacbe,* which is about 60 feet wide and runs for about a mile through the "downtown" area of the city. The buildings are situated on great plazas extending from this boulevard. Keep in mind that this entire area was once absolutely level, paved with cement, with palaces and temples rising from the plazas, and you will better sense the scope of this great city.

On your left as you enter is the STANDING TEMPLE, a small building on an extensive mound, of great antiquity and very different from any that you have seen before. Its walls are of roughly squared blocks, its corbeled vaults of great slabs. It is wholly undecorated, only an inset panel on its front frieze alters its absolute simplicity. A stair rises to nothingness beside it, having once given access to the roof or to a superposed temple. There is, by the way, considerable evidence that here at Dzibilchaltún the Mayas were their own excavators, building one temple on top of another, then, hundreds of years later, removing the upper to once again reveal the lower.

Ahead is the CENOTE XLACAH, once the center of this downtown area, a roughly oval-shaped pool with the remains of a temple marring its curved edges. During the course of time, the temple slid down into the *cenote,* providing wonderful opportunities for recent archaeological scuba divers.

As you turn east on the wide *sacbe,* on your right will be a huge plaza where a palace once stood. It is now occupied by the ruined frame of a Spanish church, one of the very earliest to be built in Yucatán. Further along the road, in its center, is a platform with a crude stele. Although all decorations have been worn away from it, it is still most impressive to see it standing starkly alone here.

The TEMPLE OF THE SEVEN DOLLS (*Siete Muñecas*) is a sheer wonder to behold, as it stands, delicate and golden, amid the vast green plain. Built about A.D. 475, it was later buried so that a greater edifice might be erected above it. Later generations reversed this procedure. With the work done by scholars from Tulane University and the National Geographic Society, in 1956, it now is exquisitely pristine. It stands on a pyramid base, rather than a platform, and is reached by a double flight of stairs separated by a niche that originally held a stele. It differs from all other structures (except the Palace at Palenque, with which it is roughly contemporaneous) in that it bears a tower, indeed, a tower with a single small window on its south side, which was doubtless used to fix some important astronomical occurrence.

Its western face has two windows that were used to light the interior. No other building in the land of the Maya possesses such a characteristic; yet, as it is an early building, it is surprising that it was not copied elsewhere.

The frieze is plain, except for the inset panel. Yet

masks center over each door and at the corners. These masks may well be primitive representations of Chac. Instead of the elaborately curved nose of the ubiquitous Rain God, thin slabs jut out at nose and chin, but the general impression is much the same.

The interior of the temple has been cleared by archaeologists, with all of its important pieces being removed to one museum or another. When originally uncovered, an altar bearing a T-shaped symbol was found, with a medallion on the symbol. In fact, there were found to be several medallions, in layers! Hieroglyphics on it date it as being the late fourteenth century, and are the only known inscriptions dating from the last centuries of Maya history!

Under the altar is a crypt that contained seven small clay figurines (dolls), each modeled to show some physical defect. A tube (called by the imaginative a "psychoduct") connected the altar with the crypt, and permitted the priest to communicate directly with the spirit world. It is noteworthy that this device is also used at Palenque, where it follows the stairs that lead from the altar of the Temple of the Inscriptions to the tomb below.

Look back as you drive away from Dzibilchaltún. See the tiny golden buildings rising above the miles of gray-green henequen spikes. Remember that you have seen here, comparatively early in its period of exploration, what may well prove to be the greatest of all the Maya cities.

Uxmal

Scholars completely disagree as to when Uxmal was established. Not only do historical data and archaeological evidence point to different dates of founding, but other scientific material fails to support either. History tells of the League of Mayapán—but Mayapán, Chichén Itzá, and Uxmal did not flourish concurrently, according to archaeology. Reputedly, Uxmal was founded by the Xiu, a Mexican tribe that invaded Yucatán at the end of the tenth century A.D. Yet most of the buildings of Uxmal were erected during and shortly after the seventh century.

Such disputes need not concern you unduly. Regardless of its background, Uxmal is a city of the Maya renaissance, whose simplicity is a thing of beauty. Its Classic style is almost pure Puuc—plain walls and decorated friezes. Such Toltec influence as exists is found in the form of overlays, the addition of Mexican symbols to already-present motifs. Here you will not find the fierceness and rapacity of tigers and eagles as you did at

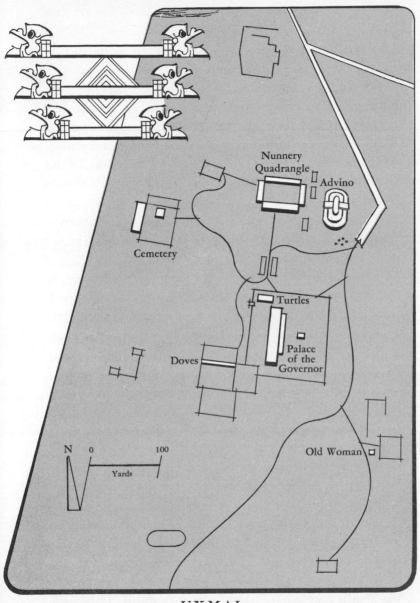

Nunnery
Quadrangle

Advino

Cemetery

Turtles

Doves

Palace
of the
Governor

N   0   100

Yards

Old Woman

UXMAL

Chichén; instead your eye will be soothed by the beauty of its line and of its ornament.

Uxmal is located in the Puuc, or hill country, a gently rolling range about an hour's drive south of Mérida. It is much more compact than Chichén Itzá, and the arrangement of its buildings can be readily comprehended. Much of its appeal lies in the beauty of the detail of the buildings themselves, rather than in the vigor of the architecture.

You will want to spend your time here, not in wandering around, but in returning to sit and look at certain sites, delighting more and more in what you see as more becomes understandable to you. Each piece of stone has a special meaning, placed deliberately exactly where it now is by the express design of architects long dead. The frieze of the Palace of the Governor is not a flat mass, embellished with decoration; instead it is an intricate mosaic, its component stones placed at different depths in order to develop a moving pattern of light and shade.

You are at once conscious of the brooding black bulk of the Pyramid of the Magician rising very steeply to your right as you enter the grounds. This is not an orderly pyramid like the Castillo at Chichén. Instead it is rough and crude, fiercely dominant and unrestrained, frightening in its towering might.

As you follow the path around its southern side, you will see a group of phalli, clustered on the ground like oversized mushrooms. These were not originally a part of this area, but were moved here from the Temple of the Phalli that lies half a mile further south. They were not intended as erotic devices, but are a fertility symbol, used in religious rites.

Perched up on the western face of the Advino, you will see the Chenes Temple, so heavily decorated with masks of Chac that it becomes a giant mask. And under the stairway that leads to it is yet another temple, using to a lesser degree the same motif.

Ahead of you lies the Nunnery Quadrangle, its four buildings perhaps the most beautiful ever constructed by the ancient Maya. Each one is distinctive, yet they form a harmonious whole. You will want to examine them carefully, to see for yourself the architects' intentions.

Walking down its south side, out through its famous corbeled archway, you pass through the narrow Ball Court, much in ruins. Ahead is the vast mound, with the long, lovely Palace of the Governor upon it. In front of the Palace is a platform bearing a two-headed Jaguar Throne. On the northwest corner of the area is the House of the Turtles, delicate and simple. Behind the Palace, at ground level and actually cut back into the mound, is a small and quite ruined Chenes temple.

From here you can see very clearly on your left the triangular roof combs of the House of the Doves, so-called because their appearance reminded the Spaniards of the dovecotes of their homeland.

Leaving the Palace by the Ball Court side, you will take a path to the left that leads into a thicket of trees; and, turning left here, you will cross a low mound to enter the Cemetery, where the skull and crossbones motif will remind you of the Tzompantli at Chichén. If you had, instead, turned right into the woods, you would come to a short path that leads left to the Platform of the Stelae, where a dozen tall stelae lie on their sides awaiting your close inspection. You may return from here directly to the rear of the west side of the Nunnery by taking a right-hand path.

You have now circled and visited the entire main area of Uxmal, and only a few outlying spots of differing degrees of interest remain.

The North Group, much ruined, is reached by a path that leads steeply to the right before you enter the grounds. The House of the Old Woman lies a short distance from a trail that passes by the east side of the mound upon which the Palace is built. Not worth climbing in itself (although it provides a lovely view from its top), it is noteworthy for the very ancient statue of an Old Woman that not one in ten thousand visitors discovers. Crudely carved, of obvious great age, she lies supine behind a small mound on the right side of the main pyramid.

If you followed the main trail instead of branching off, you would come after about half a mile to the Temple of the Phalli. This is much in ruins, and only one device remains prominent, on the south frieze. Incidentally, the view from the top of this low building stretches out over miles of treetops as the land falls away beyond and affords an eerie sense of isolation. The Chimez Temple and the arch beyond it cannot be reached today, since the jungle has wholly closed in around them, yet the temple itself may be discerned, rising above the encroaching trees, from the area of the Palace of the Governor.

You will have noticed, perhaps, that there are no *cenotes* at Uxmal, a fact that is true throughout the Puuc. To serve the needs of the ancient city, giant *aguadas* (reservoirs) were constructed, vast hollows lined with cement that stored the accumulated rainwater through the dry season. These have been deliberately destroyed as a part of a mosquito-control program, a worthwhile operation—Stephens spoke of the hordes of "moschetoes" and of the notorious reputation for disease held by the area. There are also lidded *chultunes*, one of which may readily be seen at the North Group.

THE BUILDINGS OF UXMAL

PYRAMID OF THE MAGICIAN   This structure has more names than it has temples. It is called, variously, a pyramid, a house, or a temple; and is designated as belonging to a magician (Advino), a sorcerer, a soothsayer, or a dwarf.

A legend clings to this temple, the legend of the miracle-working dwarf. It seems that an old woman succeeded in hatching a child from an egg (according to one version, the egg of a serpent). The child, at one year old, was fully grown, yet a dwarf. Challenging the king of Uxmal, he successfully performed many magical feats. The king, in anger, commanded the dwarf on pain of death to build a great palace within a single night, and this giant pyramid was the result. This success infuriated the king, who decreed a test of strength between himself and the magician. A tremendously hard nut was to be split open on the skull of each, beginning, of course, with the dwarf's. Because of a magic plate provided by the old woman, the dwarf survived; but the king perished in his turn, and the dwarf reigned in his stead. The old witch-woman is commemorated by a pyramid of her own, a bit to the south of the Magician's, and her ancient statue lies there to this day.

The pyramid is interesting in that its base is elliptical instead of having the usual squared-off corners. No less than five distinct temples are a part of it, each constructed at a different period.

The earliest of all is at ground level on the western side. Only the façade can now be seen, since the interior rooms have been filled with rubble, and even this is mostly hidden behind a broad stairway. Blank sections alternate with groups of decorative columns to give a pleasing, simple effect.

Because this lower temple was covered by the pyramid and the stairs were erected, a second temple was built in the center of the broad, flat surface at the top. This structure is no longer visible, hidden inside the extension of the pyramid that supports the uppermost temple. It may be reached, however, through the hole that you see about two thirds of the way up the eastern steps, but to do so will scarcely repay your time and effort.

The third temple is also now in the interior of the

giant pyramid, with its façade forming the rear wall of the fourth temple.

This fourth temple, accessible by the steeper, shorter west stair, is known, because of its architectural style, as the Chenes Temple, and is one of the most interesting structures of Uxmal. You will recall from your visit to Chichén Itzá that in the Chenes style the entire face of the building is decorated, whereas in the Puuc only the frieze is decorated. Here, as elsewhere when the Chenes décor is employed, the ornamentation consists of re-peated masks of Chac, reiterated until the entire face of the building, even its yawning door, becomes one gigan-tic mask. The access stair is very steep, with narrow steps and high risers, but there is a chain to assist you. The balustrade also consists of Chac masks. You will notice that these masks, on the stairs as well as on the throne on the upper level at the temple, have their noses reversed . . . no one knows why.

The fifth and last temple is reached by the broad stairs, also provided with a chain, that cover the eastern side of the pyramid. It is, unfortunately, quite dull and uninteresting, and is notable principally for the magnifi-cent view it affords of the surrounding countryside. There is a niche containing a *na* (hut) over its door-way that once probably held a stone idol, but if you are going to climb it, do so only for the view.

PALACE OF THE GOVERNOR This building, described by Sylvanus Morley as "the most magnificent, the most spectacular single building in all pre-Columbian America," stands on a natural elevation that was enlarged and smoothed to form a broad terrace. The structure itself stands upon another long, narrow platform that greatly enhances the beauty of its proportions.

On a small platform to its east is the two-headed Jaguar Throne, affording an ideal spot from which you may leisurely examine the details of the beauty of the Palace.

A pleasant little legend is connected with the two-headed jaguar. You will notice that one half is a bit larger than the other, and that the two sections are connected by a band. In ancient days, so the story goes, couples desiring to be married were brought here by the priest, for the throne represents male and female, indissolubly wedded by the ring that joins them. Whether or not this is good archaeology is open to question, but it is a happy thought that has come down over the centuries.

The Palace of the Governor originally consisted of a great central building with two small, separated wings, connected with the main palace by two very high, corbeled vaults. At a later date, this passage was blocked off by a low cross wall and a frieze in the form of a thatched hut added. (This stone "thatching" has fallen, but the work of restoring it, piece by piece, is being carried on behind the palace.)

Sit and look at the Palace of the Governor as the fluffy clouds sweep across the blue sky of Yucatán. See how the lights and shadows vary on the length of the façade. Notice that each stone, and there are some twenty thousand of them in this immense mosaic, is set at exactly the proper depth in relation to its neighbors so that there is a continuous interplay of light and shade.

Look more closely. See the pattern that underlies this sweep of beauty. It consists of garlands of masks of Chac rising and falling over stepped frets and latticed panels. Over the central doorway, all that remains of a seated figure is a magnificent feathered headdress, set against conventionalized serpent-headed bars.

HOUSE OF THE TURTLES   On the northwest corner of the main terrace of the Palace is a building notable because of "the justness and beauty of its proportions, the chasteness and simplicity of its ornament," to quote Stephens once again.

Its sole decoration is a frieze consisting of close-packed small columns, on the cornice above which are a row of turtles in full relief. A feeling of peace comes as you look at this small, simple building, so reminiscent of the temples of Classical Greece.

The turtle is a common decorative theme of the Maya. You will be able to discern it with some frequency, once you have become conscious of its religious importance. The reason is that the turtle leads an amphibious existence, at home in two elements, and as such was considered to provide a clue to combined life in the present world and in the world of the spirit. For, as you have seen at Dzibilchaltún and will see at Palenque, the priests believed in communication between these two worlds.

HOUSE OF THE DOVES   This spectacular façade forms only part of a complex which, when further exploration is done, may well turn out to be as important as the Nunnery, whose plan it closely resembles. As it now stands, the triangular roof combs, resembling dovecotes, may be satisfactorily viewed from a distance.

If you wish to examine it more closely, climb on the rubble to the northeast corner of the building and you can look down into a huge courtyard, backed by the South Pyramid and flanked by the Great Pyramid. The far side of the square is a ruined building. Walking around the east rim to the south side, you will find that the roof of this building forms a courtyard itself, and that, looking north, you can see through a vaulted passage like the one at the Nunnery.

Climbing the adjacent pyramids is essentially unrewarding. There are the remains of structures upon them, but much is buried or broken, and the decorative motifs that remain visible merely repeat those you have seen elsewhere.

CEMETERY   Leaving the terrace of the Palace of the Governor by a path near the House of the Turtles, follow the path to the left into the trees, and then turn left and cross a small mound to enter the Cemetery.

On your right as you enter is a low platform that will at once remind you of the Tzompantli, for it is decorated with a row of skulls and crossbones. It is a great deal lower, and the motif is cut below a line of glyphs, but the elements are remarkably clear.

There are two curious—and unexplained—elements in the Cemetery area. One is that the corner heads on the platform are carved upside-down, and are not the conventional death's-head, but rather may represent a feathered bird. Kukulcán? But why upside-down? The other is a monolith, carved into three conjoined rings, that appears to be an altar at the left side of the area. No one has yet hazarded a guess as to its significance.

The third side of the square area is occupied by a small plain temple, apparently once decorated with stucco figures, for you can see the remaining stone protuberances.

PLATFORM OF THE STELAE   Following your original path to the right, you come into a thicket and climb a short grade. A path leads a little distance into the woods on the left, and comes out in a cleared area where the stelae, long, flat monoliths 5 to 10 feet long, are lying on their sides, just as they were placed so that Morley, the distinguished archaeologist, could better study them.

While most have been fairly well effaced by the weather, two or three are most interesting to examine. One shows a priest, almost obliterated by a gigantic feather headdress, surrounded by masked mythological figures, standing upon a jaguar throne that rests, in its turn, on the bodies of two naked men, with abnormally large penises.

From this area follow your path a short distance to the east, and you will emerge from the woods at the northwest corner of the Nunnery.

NUNNERY QUADRANGLE   Entering the great courtyard of the Nunnery (it measures about 70 by 50 yards), you will see a pile of stones in its approximate center. Stephens describes such a pile as "of uncouth and irregular proportions, wanting conformity with the regularity and symmetry of all around. From its conspicuous position, it doubtless has some important use, and induces the belief that it was connected with the ceremonial rites of an ancient worship known to have existed among all Eastern nations. The Indians call this stone the Picote, or whipping post."

Aside from that, this broken stone makes a wonderful place to sit and rest while you inspect more closely each of the very different buildings that compose the Quadrangle. Each structure is very distinct architecturally from its neighbor; and, as they represent a progression from the simple to the ornate, you may wish to look at them in detail in that order.

The SOUTH BUILDING provided the main entrance to the group, by means of a broad stairway which led up from the Ball Court. The corbel-vaulted passage is exceptionally graceful, and affords a fine view of the House of the Turtles and the Palace in the background. Flanking this passage, above the doors to the rooms, are peasant huts, each topped by a mask of Chac. The lattice-

paneled frieze upon which these are mounted represents
the mats used in making temples before stone construction was possible. The simplicity and lovely proportions
of this building are especially notable.

You will be interested, too, when you go out through
the passage, to see on the vault the marks of the red
hand, left there, as in the Akab-Dzib at Chichén, by reverent masons a thousand years ago.

The EAST BUILDING, if possible, is even more lovely
than its neighbor to the south. Once again you will see
the lattice used as the background of the frieze, but the
main decoration consists of six trapezoids of eight bars
each, representing double-headed serpents. Mounted on
each of these is the head of an owl. Over the central door
and at the corners are triple masks of Chac.

The NORTH BUILDING is the largest of the four, rising
from a platform dominating the area. At ground level,
flanking the broad stair, are two smaller temples, the left-
hand one of which, the Temple of Venus, is notable for
the double columns that support its wide entrance.

In the center of steps between the two lower temples
is a squat stele, covered with a pattern of squared hieroglyphs. These do not date the area, but were more probably in commemoration of some important event.

Over its doors, thatched huts alternate with masks of
Chac, piled four high into turrets projecting above the
roof line. Between, against panels of large latticework
and of stepped frets, are most interesting carved figures.
There is a prisoner, bound with ropes; a kneeling man;

a flute player . . . and the most charmingly plump little owl you'll ever see. And you will enjoy walking
around the building to discover other engaging sights.
The two-headed jaguar over the central doorway was
probably added at a later date, as a tie-in with that in
front of the Palace of the Governor.

The decoration on the frieze of the WEST BUILDING is
highly complex, and you can readily see that much of it
was added to a simple latticework–Chac masks original.
Indeed, with its interplay of frets and bands, it must
once have greatly resembled the North Building in this
respect. Here, too, are found the thatched huts and the
piled masks.

Over the principal doorway is a magnificent feathered
throne, on which a queer figure is seated: the head of an
old man surmounts the body of a turtle. Despite its obvious importance, its significance is unknown.

Now you will suddenly see the added element, the
feathered serpent of the Toltecs, two of them in fact,
coiling and winding over the lattice and beneath the
masks. Follow one long, sinuous body with your eye. It
begins with a yawning mouth, a human head in its gap-
ing jaws. Over and under the stone the body writhes, to
return to a place on the frieze above the reptile's head.
The tail has a hanging rattle, but upon it is the Plant of
Life, its curling flower rising from it.

Also added, centering on Greek keys, are various
human figures, each with an animal head on the panel
above it. These bodies represent priests and warriors,

but some are naked, and exhibit gross, tattooed penises, as do the slaves supporting the priest on the stele.

You will want to return more than once to this courtyard of the Nunnery, to savor its serene beauty as well as to study the fascinating details.

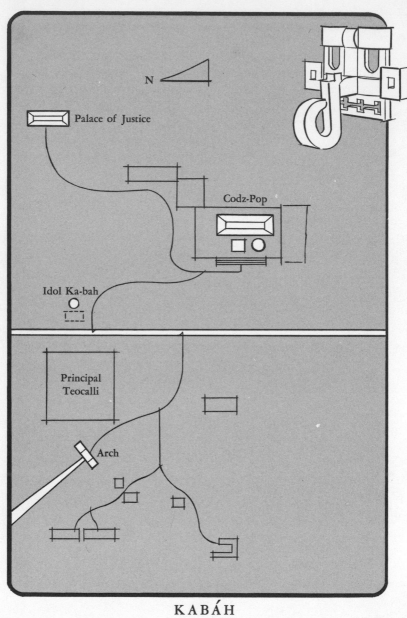

N

Palace of Justice

Codz-Pop

Idol Ka-bah

Principal
Teocalli

Arch

KABÁH

Kabáh

Kabáh lies about twelve miles south of Uxmal on the main highway to Campeche. On the way, you will pass a sign on your right reading "Ruinas Mulchic." At this site not long ago were found frescoes judged to be the peers of those at Bonampak. However, in order better to preserve them, they have been removed by the Mexican government, and will later be exhibited at the magnificent Archaeological Museum in Mexico City; so the ruins are just ruins now.

One hundred and twenty-five years after John Lloyd Stephens came to Kabáh, he still remains the most accurate observer of the area. He saw the ruins with a sympathetic yet practical eye, discovering in them much of great interest and importance.

The first building that meets your eye is the gigantic mound which Stephens designated as the PRINCIPAL TEOCALLI, a truncated pyramid which once bore on its summit a temple, now mostly a huge mound of rubble. It is a tough climb up it, as its steps and terraces are decayed, and there is only a view of endless jungle to reward you.

After parking your car near the Teocalli, cross the road to the office at the gate house and enter the area there. Be sure that you do not miss the idol on the far side of the house. This crudely carved stone figure, depicting a kneeling man with a serpent, was discovered in the Principal Teocalli, and was moved here for safekeeping. It is called Ka-bah, a Mayan word meaning "The Man with the Ax." Stephens, by the way, did not see this idol, which was, in his time, still buried within the mound.

On a very broad terrace to your right is the CODZ-POP, the magnificent TEMPLE OF THE MASKS. And that is exactly what it is, for its entire façade, from roof comb to pediment, from end to end, is an endless repetition of long-snouted representations of Chac. This is grander than the small cube of a Chenes temple; it is Maya baroque. The use of this motif is so lavish that it is simply overwhelming. Mask and mask and mask are repeated until the entire surface seems to shimmer.

Codz-Pop means "rolled mat" and refers to the fact that both the exterior and interior steps of the building feature the curved Chac nose. In other temples that you have seen, both interior rooms have been on the same floor level. Here the rear rooms are a couple of feet higher, and are reached by stepping on the broad nose of a giant mask of Chac, first on the curved area, then on the flat projection, before you take a final step up to his head at the rear room's floor level. It seems quite possible, too, that these mask-steps were also used as a throne, where a seated priest could be flanked by his retainers.

On the outer terrace of this fascinating building are, at the present time, hundreds of fragments of carved columns, which are being matched by archaeologists to restore them to their rightful place on the ruined mound just to the south. Also in front of the Codz-Pop is a great, flat cemented area, feeding rainwater into a giant *chultun* that underlies the terrace. There is also a square altar platform whose sides are composed of square-cut stones carved with elaborate glyphs. Perhaps this was originally built to display a two-headed jaguar, since it closely resembles the platform in front of the Palace of the Governor at nearby Uxmal.

Behind the Codz-Pop is a building which the Indians of Stephens' day called the *cocina,* or kitchen, because they thought that the two apertures at its top were chimneys to let out smoke. These "chimneys," which suggest more the eyes or tufted ears of an owl, are really the exposed ends of the corbel-vaulted rooms of an upper temple that once stood at right angles to the Codz-Pop.

The broad stair that leads up to this building is built over a passage like that of the Temple of the Wall Panels at Chichén, but instead of being a full corbeled vault, it is only half of one. This structure is a very handsome one; the simple frieze is broken by bundles of decorative columns. You will note that two of its doors are wider than the others, and are supported at the center by a column with a Doric capital. This is, so to speak, a "working" column, a functional one in that it actually permits the use of two lintel stones, a feature that is rare in Maya architecture.

Leaving this platform by its north side, a short trail leads back into the woods. Beside it you will see a number of smaller *chultunes,* each, luckily, carefully covered. A hundred yards or so in is a building called, for no particular reason, the PALACE OF JUSTICE.

You will first catch a glimpse of this lovely building through a gap in the trees, as it gleams whitely in the sunlight. The wall of this temple carries a simple decoration, for the space between the doors has a panel of columns. The entire frieze is faced with columns as well, with a narrow median cornice bearing a conventionalized serpent band.

Crossing the main road once again, and leaving the Principal Teocalli on your right, you will follow a broad path across the fields to the now-famous ARCH OF KABÁH. Unfortunately it has been so over-restored that it has to a great degree lost its majesty. No longer will you feel the sense of awe amid desolation that it once evoked in its ruined state. It may, perhaps, be easier to recognize it as a triumphal arch, commemorating a now-forgotten victory, but its neatly arranged stones have lost the grandeur that they formerly held. However, the brush has been cleared away from its vicinity, and you can now see very clearly that it spans a sacred road that links Kabáh with Uxmal.

You have now seen all the important structures, but
if time permits, you may enjoy further retracing Stephens' steps, even though the discoveries which he made
are no longer *in situ*.

Before you came to the Arch, you will have noticed a
path leading into the woods to the left. After a short distance, this path splits. First, as Stephens did, follow the
right fork down his "pathway to the *milpas*." Here you
come to two small plain buildings set at right angles to
each other. It was in this patio, while Stephens was investigating further on foot, that his tethered horse
slipped into a pit, to be extricated only with great difficulty. Be careful!

Passing between these two buildings, a path runs back
into denser woods toward the TEMPLE OF THE SCULP-
TURED BEAM, and another called now La Grecque because of its simplicity. Both are in ruins now; and the
original wooden beams were removed by Stephens, later
to be destroyed by a fire at his New York museum.

If you had taken the left fork earlier, you would have
come out on a large *milpa* at the small building where
Stephens found an ornament in stucco (with a large
hornet's nest attached), which appeared to him to represent two eagles facing each other. Alas, this, too, has disappeared, although Stephens—perhaps because of the
hornet's nest—did not disturb it. On the far side of the
field is another larger temple, whose beautifully carved
stone jambs are now in the Museum of Natural History
in New York City.

Not a very rewarding walk? Perhaps not, but there is a certain thrill in knowing that you have followed exactly the steps of that master storyteller of one hundred and twenty-five years ago.

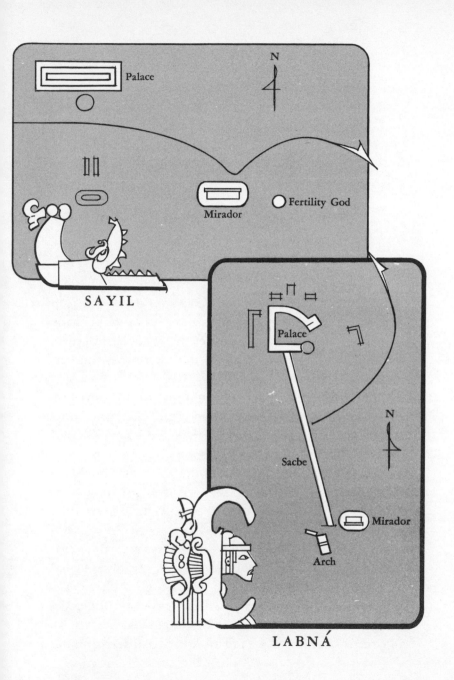

SAYIL

LABNÁ

Labná, Sayil, and X-lapahk

These cities are reached in the course of an all-day jeep trip into the back country of Yucatán. It cannot be made by private car or without a guide: the roads are too rutty for any but a high-slung vehicle, and there are innumerable possibilities for getting lost.

The road is rough—unbelievably so. And you will return to your hotel at sundown good and tired after your 7 A.M. start and your day of clinging to the stanchions of the jeep. If you have a bad back, don't take the trip.

Arrangements for this out-of-the-way tour should be made at the Hacienda Uxmal. As you might expect, there are only a limited number of vehicles available; and in the crowded season, seating capacity gets pretty tight. If at all possible, try to go on a day with as few others as possible, since this will permit greater personal attention from the guides. If you do go with a large group, try to get your seats in a car driven by either the head guide or his son, both of whom are extremely well-informed on Maya lore and philosophical background.

Other drivers are just that, no more, and cannot be expected to answer your innumerable questions. With the help of the experienced guides, you will emerge from the trip with a real appreciation of the Maya people, and a knowledge of their daily lives that goes far beyond the mere seeing of archaeological areas.

There is also, by the way, a safari that takes you camping out at Labná overnight. Here you sleep, as did Stephens, in a hammock slung in an ancient temple; and eat native dishes prepared for you by your Indian guide. Insect repellent has removed much of the discomfort that the pioneer explorer underwent; and the sight of the jungle ruins by starlight is unforgettable.

Whether you go by day or spend the night as well, your trip will be a fascinating and original experience; for the cities are lovely, and different in style from others that you have seen in the Puuc.

Your route takes you on the main road to a short distance past Kabáh, where you turn left into the jungle itself. Nearby, at a beekeeper's hut, is the disused Well of Chack. Here, after entering a cave, low, narrow crevices once led for a quarter mile underground to a depth of 450 feet to a source of water. As Stephens said—and he went down and examined it in 1840—this was the only source of water during the dry season for an area of "three leagues" (nine miles) around. Town wells, such as you see today, with stone sides and a rope and bucket, dried up during the height of the dry season; modern well-drilling, pumps, and windmills have, of course, changed all this.

The road in to these Maya cities is narrow and rocky, and the jeep plunges and bucks like a horse as it slips and slides along. Keep your arms inboard, for a shrub called *cuernos del toro* (horns of the bull) grows thickly beside the road—and you will be aware of its long, black, sharp thorns.

You will first come out on the clearing of Sayil, with its magnificent hundred-room Palace. Nearby, behind the towering height of the Mirador, a crude fertility idol is half-hidden. These are sights that you will not find elsewhere, and you will be greatly interested.

Shortly after leaving Sayil, you will enter the great plantation of Sabachtsché, a cattle-ranching area that stretches over much of this portion of the Puuc. Here, in the cleared *milpas* beside the road, are the ruins of the ancient city of the same name. Little is left of it now, trees and vines tear apart the buildings; but the scene of desolation is unforgettable.

All that you will see of X-lapahk is a single temple by the trail, overhung with jungle. It has been deliberately left in its present condition in order that you may see it as Stephens saw it, its beauty all the more appealing because of its wildness. This building (the name X-lapahk means Ruined Walls) was built in A.D. 850 of stone mosaic, as contrasted to the larger blocks of older buildings. Masks of Chac compose its corners, while its frieze is of delicate decorative columns. Its lower cornice is split by short columns to give it a delicate touch.

Labná is in a large clearing, bisected by a raised *sacbe*. Three principal structures are seen here: a lovely Palace, the famous Arch of Labná and its adjacent walls, and, as at Sayil, a Mirador with a spectacular roof comb.

After starting your return trip, shortly after repassing Sabachtsché, you will take a right-hand fork that you had not noticed on your way in. By now you will have become accustomed to the bucking of the jeep, and think that maybe the roughness isn't as bad as its anticipation. You will now discover how wrong you were. Where the road has been unbelievably rough, it now becomes impossibly so; and you will cling and brace yourself as your expert driver maneuvers over a trail that appears impassable.

Fields open up on either side, and you pass the gates of the Hacienda Santa Ana, with its towering factory chimney (where sugar was once refined) and its small Spanish church. And soon thereafter you will return to civilization, coming out on the main road just north of Kabáh.

You'll be tired, certainly. But you will have gained in your knowledge and appreciation of the Maya cities by having spent a day seeing sights that the average traveler just does not take the time to see. You will have traveled off the beaten path; seen *milpas* in various stages of cultivation, and have come to recognize more of the daily life of the Maya people as it is lived today—almost exactly as their ancestors lived more than a thousand years ago.

You will have become conscious of the inexorable sequence of the life cycle of the Maya. And you will speculate perhaps, with firsthand knowledge, on the cause of desertion by the Maya of their great stone cities. You will wonder if it was the exhaustion of the land surrounding them, so that peasants could no longer support themselves—and dense populations of non-productive priests and nobles—that caused whole people to move en masse to a virgin area, building new temples and palaces that were in turn claimed by the jungle.

SAYIL

As is the case in all Maya cities, you are only seeing a small fraction of the number of buildings that once existed. Sayil, or Place of the Ants, is named from the number of mounds in the area.

The GREAT PALÁCE, containing over a hundred rooms, was erected over a span of some one hundred and fifty years, between A.D. 700 and 850. As you can see, it doesn't exactly match. The lower east wing is similar but not identical to that of the lower west. With its three stories, it is a magnificent building, possessing (as Victor von Hagen wrote) "magnitude, proportion, order, sensibleness."

You will be struck here by the close resemblance of its detail to Greek Doric architecture, for the twin columns supporting the broad doorways have distinctively Doric capitals. On the center (and most rewarding) level, the wall is decorated with bundles of superficial columns. It is on this tier, too, that the frieze is exceptionally lovely, completely different from any you have seen before.

Over the central broad row of decorative columns
(Stephens speaks of them as being "curiously orna-
mented," but they are really plain with a central band
corresponding to their capital and base) is an exceptionally fine Chac mask; the great fangs almost reach over a
lower cornice split by stubby columns. Similar Chac
masks are found, as usual, at the corners of the building.

Over the small doors are alligators (or scorpions?)
with upraised tails and open jaws, flanking a Diving
God such as you will see at Tulúm. Stephens writes that
it "is the figure of a man supporting himself on his
hands, with his legs expanded in a curious rather than
a delicate attitude."

A short distance away, concealed in trees, the
MIRADOR rises from a large mound. Stephens' description of his first sight of it is interesting. "In front of the
Casa Grande, at a distance of five hundred yards is another structure, strikingly different from any we had
seen, more strange and inexplicable, and having at a distance the appearance of a New England factory."

What gave it this appearance—and it really is a most
apt comparison—is its tremendously high roof comb,
pierced with holes to reduce windage. The structure is
otherwise plain and uninteresting; but the comb, once
decorated with stucco statues as at Palenque, is highly
striking.

To the left of the Mirador, now supine on the ground
of the patio, is a bas-relief figure of a fertility god with a
gigantic phallus.

In addition to numerous stelae (which are now in the

Archaeological Museum in Mexico City), Stephens reports on several other buildings in Sayil. At present, none of these are accessible until further restoration is accomplished.

LABNÁ

Once a large and important ceremonial center, much of Labná is today still hidden in the jungle. Yet the portion that is visible you will find enchanting and, again, different from other cities of the Puuc, yet possessing common characteristics with them.

Built in A.D. 869 (as can be told by the hieroglyphs on one of the Chac masks) Labná today consists of three principal edifices: a lovely Palace; a towering Mirador; and a finely designed Arch; plus a raised *sacbe* that crosses the center of the cleared area.

As you enter from the direction of Sayil, you will cross the *sacbe* and swing right to the PALACE. (Stephens had such a high opinion of this building that Frederick Catherwood, who sketched the Maya cities for Stephens, placed it as the frontispiece to the second volume of *Incidents of Travel in Yucatán*.) The Palace was composed of several buildings built at different periods in slightly different styles; its principal façade is simply decorated, not only on its frieze but on the wall itself.

Again you see columns used decoratively, not as weight-bearing members, but to these have been added panels with a woven appearance that is highly original. Once again you will see, too, as you have noticed on so many buildings in the Puuc, that the whole structure is carried on a base composed of short, stubby columns, a motif that is, in some parts, used on the cornice as well.

The frieze makes extensive use of the "Greek key," interspersed at intervals with bundles of columns and embellished with masks of Chac. On one corner, nearest to the Chac whose nose bears the date hieroglyphs, is a magnificent sculpture of the open jaws of an alligator, enclosing a human head that is reminiscent of, but perhaps more delicately beautiful than, the ones you have seen on the Temple of the Warriors in Chichén or of the famous "Queen of Uxmal" (now in Mexico City).

In front of the Palace are huge *chultunes* into one of which Stephens had himself lowered. At the foot of the terrace is a tree, the very same "noble ramon" whose life Stephens spared because of its majestic appearance. These trees served as fodder for horses and cattle, and the Indians of his day had standing orders from the owner of the *rancho* not to cut them down.

Across the plaza is the MIRADOR, built on a mound with rounded corners as is the Advino at Uxmal. Its gigantic roof comb was once decorated with major stucco sculptures, thus providing contrast to its plain facade. This comb still stands intact today, although Stephens, a very adventurous man, did not climb it because it was then (1841) "tottering and about to fall."

The ARCH OF LABNÁ is not a separate, monumental structure (as is Kabáh's), but served once as the entrance way to a patio or courtyard. In this respect it resembles the passage through the South Building of the Nunnery at Uxmal. Like it, too, on its interior it bears representations of the thatched peasant hut; the exterior carries columns and Greek keys. At the left, in the interior court, is an exceptionally lovely stretch of wall that has recently been restored; its decoration is composed of columns of various lengths arranged in a most harmonious relationship. When you are dining in the Hacienda Uxmal you will see on, or rather, set into the wall of the dining room, an excellent carved wooden replica of this lovely area.

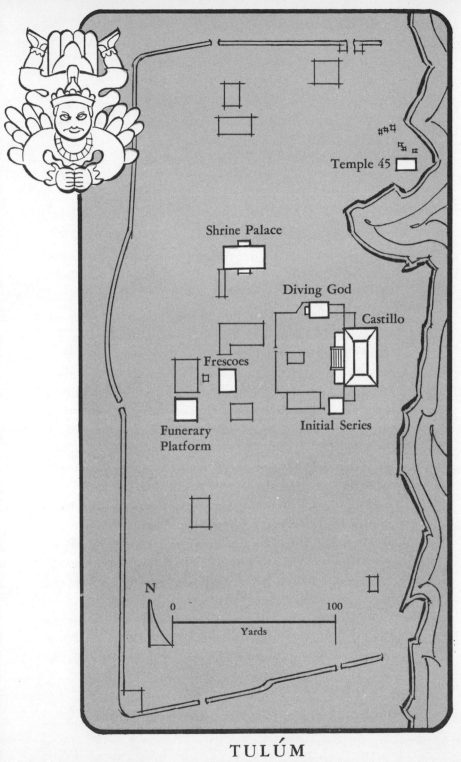

Temple 45

Shrine Palace

Diving God

Castillo

Frescoes

Funerary
Platform

Initial Series

N

0   100

Yards

TULÚM

Tulúm

It was the Year of Our Lord 1518. The fleet under the command of Juan de Grijalva was working its way slowly along the Caribbean coast of Yucatán (the present territory of Quintana Roo) when the eye of a lookout was caught by the gleam of white buildings shining in the evening sun. It was the first glimpse that these bearded *conquistadores* had of the walled city of Tulúm, described by Grijalva himself as "a bourg or village so large that Seville itself would not have appeared larger or better."

In common with most explorers, Don Juan was exaggerating a bit. What he was really describing was a sort of Maya megalopolis that runs for several miles along the palisaded coast. Tulúm itself was not large enough to warrant such a flowery phrase, but it was a major Maya ceremonial site nonetheless.

Three hundred and twenty-five years passed before John Lloyd Stephens, the ubiquitous Maya explorer, heard of it from a friend who owned the nearby planta-

tion of Tancah. And when Stephens reached it, by sail-
boat from Cozumel, the site was so overgrown that it was
almost impossible to distinguish the various buildings.

Your first view of Tulúm will be very different from
that of your predecessors; a view, in fact, undoubtedly
beyond their imaginings. For you will fly here by Aero-
safari plane from Cozumel.

Sweeping in over the clear blue crystalline sea, you will
follow a white beach backed by a rough cliff perhaps
thirty-five or forty feet high. Then, on a rounded pro-
montory, will be the greenish-gray stone bulk of the
Castillo, looking inland toward a squarish court. A hundred yards on each side, north and south, are two small
temples close by the cliff end of a low stone wall.

Your plane will sweep over these quickly, turn, and
make a pass at the landing strip at Tancah before setting
down finally in the grass. This is the same Tancah plantation where Stephens stayed, and the same rough, yet
hospitable accommodations of a hammock and mosquito
net are still available should you wish to spend the night.

It is about a mile of easy walking from the strip to
Tulúm, but a jeep is ready to take you there, and you
will have plenty of exercise climbing over the site itself.
And time is always all too short. See the city first, then
walk back to the plane if you feel like it.

While you will enter Tulúm through an entrance in
the wall close by the Cenote House, you should first go
to the courtyard of the Castillo to be sure to see the most
interesting part of the city first. Since you come in
through a narrow gap in the platform-like enclosure,

climb the squarish pile of stones directly in front of you; and, sitting on its eastern side, look at the Castillo. You are now sitting on the Dance Platform, in the same place where Frederick Catherwood drew his magnificent illustration.

You will, however, see far more than he did. For, not only has the encroaching jungle been cleared away, and a considerable amount of restoration been done, but archaeologists have studied the building so that, through their aid, you can see it as it was originally, as well as recognize the alterations that have been made.

As you look at the Castillo, exercise your imagination. First, in your mind strip off the upper temple and most of the stairs leading to it. Remove, too, the twin smaller temples at ground level. Now you have left the original Castillo, a nine-columned, flat-roofed building possessing a simple beauty.

But the Mayas delighted in putting one temple on top of another, so they filled in the center section of the original, extended the stairway, and built a new, square structure there. These were the Maya-Toltecs, for the two central columns of the upper temple are the familiar serpent that you saw in the Temple of the Warriors at Chichén Itzá: head flat on the ground, jaws agape; the snake's body itself forming the massive column; and the recurved, upright rattles rising to support the lintel. The doorways are topped by three niches that once held images of the Diving God with a sun symbol. Remnants of masks adorn the corners.

Finally, but not much later, "twin" temples were

built, flanking the stairway at ground level. Despite the
fact that the roof of the northern one has fallen in, you
will see readily that these temples are not twins, but
rather resemble those in the court of the Nunnery at
Uxmal. Although they do resemble each other, the
north one had a beam and mortar roof; the south one
has a corbeled vault that has well withstood the passage
of the centuries.

Here, as you look more closely at your first building in
Tulúm, you will be conscious of certain architectural
distinctions that are characteristic throughout the city.
First, of course, are the flat, beam and mortar roofs. Not
that the corbeled vault is missing, but most of the buildings were not constructed that way. As you go about,
you will also note a peculiar vaulting that greatly resembles a "neckless bottle"; you haven't seen this elsewhere, yet it is prevalent here. Second, the outer walls
of the temples slant outward, a characteristic known as
batter, and which is so strongly evident in some buildings that they almost appear to topple outward. This
batter is accentuated in many cases by the inward sloping doorjambs. . . . Sometimes you'll think that the
temples are on the verge of collapse, when they are only
meant to be that way!

And there is the Descending God, or the Diving God.
The latter title sounds less celestial, but is more descriptive. For the figure looks just like a swimmer doing a
belly-whopper. Head up, arms akimbo, knees bent, and
feet wide, the god plunges down toward earth. This curious creature decorates the façade of almost every

building in Tulúm, and even has a special temple named after him. You will recall seeing him once before, at the Palace in Sayil.

The art of Tulúm, and there are several fine murals here, is a fascinating blend of Mixtec influences portraying Mayan religious ceremonies. Practically the whole pantheon of the Mayas is shown in one fresco or another, but the familiar gods and goddesses are so transmuted by Mexican eyes and hands that you will have to recognize them all over again.

Leave your comfortable perch on the DANCE PLATFORM, and climb the principal temples. Start on your left with the TEMPLE OF THE DIVING GOD, a small building that opens to the west, and is set on the filled-in remains of an older temple. Over the principal door is an image of the god himself, in all his serene ungracefulness, in a niche on a frieze. The frieze was once of painted rosettes, below which, on the façade, are the remnants of a once-vivid mural. Now you can hardly make out the intertwined serpents that mark the wall into blocks, within which gods and goddesses once disported themselves.

There are better preserved murals inside. A panel on the east wall shows a complex offering rite, being conducted under a band of scattered stars representing the night sky. Just to the left of the center line is our old friend, Chac, but so dressed up in Mexican uniform that you'll only recognize him by his nose. Facing him, seated on a throne, is probably the young Maize God. A symbol of life springs from his headdress, and he holds a staff in his hands.

When you come out of this temple, climb the CASTILLO. There is nothing particular to see, except that all three types of roof supports are demonstrated, but climb it. Look out across the blue Caribbean, feel the breeze in your face, and perhaps you will see the white sails of the ships of Juan de Grijalva standing out to sea.

The TEMPLE OF THE INITIAL SERIES balances, architecturally, that of the Diving God. There is no reason for entering it, for only the altar that once held Stele 1 remains. It was this stele that once gave rise to so many incorrect interpretations of the age of Tulúm. It bears the date 564 A.D., and is sculptured in the style of that period, and hence must have been brought to Tulúm rather than dedicated here.

For, with the possible exception of two buildings (one with a roof comb) outside the walls, Tulúm is a Post-Classic city, probably having been built in the thirteenth century, at a time of strong Mexican influence.

This dating is confirmed by Stele 2, which you will find on the "street" outside the Temple of the Frescoes. This stele is dated in the "Short Count" as 2 Ahau, and is identified by its somewhat decadent style as being of A.D. 1263. (The Short Count is comparable to reading '63 and guessing by its appearance to what century it belonged.)

The TEMPLE OF THE FRESCOES is probably the most interesting building in Tulúm, not for its architecture, which is generally undistinguished, but for the truly extraordinary murals that it contains. The reason for their generally excellent state of preservation is that they were painted in an interior temple over which, at a later date, another was built, thus keeping the inner chamber relatively watertight.

The frescoes themselves are of a gorgeous greenish-blue color, with tawny embellishments. Their subject is again gods and goddesses, involved in various offering ceremonies. As elsewhere in Tulúm, there is the strong Mexican influence over the Maya religious themes. One block (for the device of framing scenes by intertwined serpents is used here, too) shows the goddess Ix Chel, the patron of medicine, carrying an image of Chac in each hand.

Both the original temple and its superposition were profusely decorated with murals and painted stucco figures. As elsewhere, the Diving God was the central theme, being poised above each doorway; and, on the outside gallery, flanked by two figures in high head-dresses.

A bit to the south is the FUNERARY PLATFORM with its grave in the shape of a cross. Aside from this coincidence (for the cross has been a symbol in virtually every religion) you will be amused to learn of the diet that was provided for the dead on their journey to the next world, as exemplified by the remains of food offerings found in this tomb: shark, catfish, iguana, crocodile, dove, turkey, heron, wild pig, and sea snail!

If time is pressing at all, there is no need for you to

enter the GREAT PALACE, whose only interest lies in its curious X-barred windows, but go instead directly to the Shrine Palace to its north.

At the SHRINE PALACE, above an interior door, is a truly magnificent polychrome stucco figure of the Diving God, with most of its brilliant colors still remaining. Notice, too, the feeling of spaciousness achieved by the lack of interior columns. (The column and pillar now there were later additions, put in to prevent collapse.) The building has not been named for any noteworthy sculpture (such as the beautiful Temple of the Cross or Temple of the Sun at Palenque), but simply because of its placement. For the shrine, the holy of holies, instead of being isolated against a rear interior wall, is readily reached by direct access from the outside.

Cut from here to TEMPLE 45, on the point of land above a sandy beach to the north of the Castillo. Not that this building itself has anything to recommend it, but you will want to see the cluster of tiny oratories that are nearby. They are tiny little cubes, scarcely three feet high, and they probably once housed idols. In fact, this area may have been the center of a special fertility cult, for two stone phalli, as well as several unidentifiable sculptured objects, are found here. It was these tiny temples, of course, that gave rise to legends of hunchbacks and dwarfs, and which still plague the scholar who is seriously investigating the ancient Maya.

Returning to the wall, you will notice that it is a most peculiar fortification indeed. For some reason, on neither north nor south does it reach to the cliff's edge.

There is speculation that, for defensive purposes, a wooden barrier was fitted into these two ends, but there is no really satisfactory reason advanced as to why the gap is so very large.

At the spot where you entered Tulúm proper, the gate is flanked by two "guard rooms." This point marks the beginning of a *sacbe* that once ran up the coast to Xelha, the next main town of this coastal megalopolis.

The CENOTE HOUSE is pretty unattractive, for it really does not house a *cenote* but an *aguada:* a drainage basin and water-storage point for the city area. Scummy and befouled with bat droppings, it is best left to others to examine.

Time to go! Back to your plane!

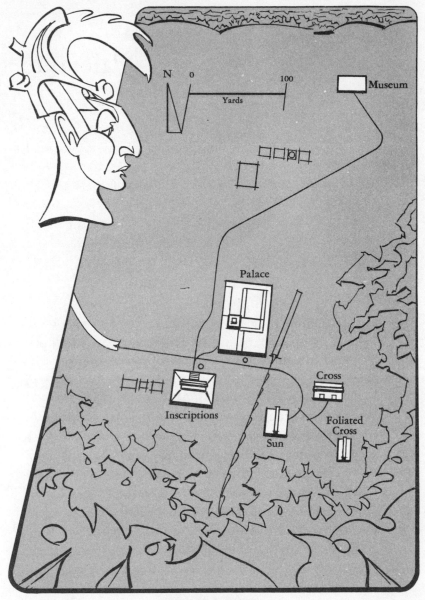

PALENQUE

Palenque

Palenque is unique.

Palenque is utterly, indescribably beautiful.

Located on a plateau a thousand feet above sea level, in a rain-forest jungle, its temples are set against a background of steeply rising, bottle-green, wooded slopes. They open out upon a vista that stretches over mile upon mile of treetops, far into the distant blue line of the horizon that is the Gulf of Mexico.

Palenque is said to be reminiscent of Angkor Wat, in the Cambodian jungle. Indeed, some archaeologists have professed to find a connection between the cities and their cultures, starting with Baron Waldeck in 1832, when he painted his deliberately "orientalized" representations in the Temple of the Lion. But, as Louis Freund has said, "the greater miracle is that there is *not* a connection between the works of art that arose almost simultaneously in Asia and in Mexico; but rather that man reached almost identical artistic expressions without contact or knowledge."

Palenque is the earliest of the cities that you have thus far seen. Hieroglyphic panels set its date at no later than A.D. 642. Yet in its stucco work—as contrasted, say, to the stone mosaic of Uxmal—Palenque has no peer in any other Maya city; and it ranks with the greatest in the world.

Of all the mysterious Maya cities, Palenque is perhaps the most mysterious. It flowered luxuriantly for some three centuries . . . and then ceased to exist. Why, no one knows. Even its very existence remained unknown for four hundred years, until as late as 1773, when an Indian told a wandering priest of its wonders. Yet Cortés and his *conquistadores,* marching to conquer and subdue Mexico, passed by only sixty miles away. As Stephens cried, "In the romance of the world's history, nothing ever impressed me more forcibly than the spectacle of this once great and lovely city, overturned, desolate and lost." (Stephens really did get around! Prior to his Yucatán travels, in 1838, he and his companion, Catherwood, landed in Guatemala and worked their way up the interior, visiting scores of Maya ruins before emerging at Palenque and going on to Uxmal.)

"It would have been difficult to choose"—writes Alberto Ruz Lhuillier, the discoverer of the tomb in the Temple of the Inscriptions—"a more appropriate place for a work worthy of the gods." This is indeed true: for natural beauty and majesty no place in the land of the Maya can compare with this mountain city; and for delicacy of sculptural detail, Palenque has no equal.

The rutted road from the present-day town of Palenque winds up the mountain side to emerge on the edge of a cleared plateau. Inquire at the gatehouse for the times that the museum and the interior of the Temple of the Inscriptions (the Funerary Crypt) will be open. Both are "musts" on your list, and as much time as possible should be allotted to each.

As you enter the grounds, there are three small temples on low mounds to your right; then you are immediately conscious of the imposing dark bulk of the Temple of the Inscriptions and the lift of the striking Palace tower.

The cloudless blue sky is above you; on your right the dark green jungle rises steeply; you feel the space that exists, that the lovely buildings are separate entities, each taking advantage of natural hills to maintain its own individuality within a common architectural style.

As a general plan for your day, you will do well to start in the morning by exploring the great Palace, a complex of buildings that is built on a centrally located high mound. In addition to seeing some of the finest stucco sculpture that the world has ever produced, you will also grasp the relative positions of the various important buildings of Palenque. The word "important" is used here to imply degree of restoration, for Palenque was a huge city, and buildings are spread over a wide area, only a small portion of which has been cleared and studied.

Then visit the museum (having checked to be certain your schedule coincides with its open hours). Here you will see perhaps the finest exhibition of local Maya antiquities that exists; many of the most beautiful and delicate pieces that have been discovered in various buildings are on display.

Under normal conditions you should visit the Funerary Crypt of the Temple of the Inscriptions next, but, because of the heavy dew, the steps, both exterior and interior, are likely to be pretty slippery until afternoon. So you had better put this off until later.

Instead, before lunch, circle the Palace, crossing the Río Otulum (only a small brook) and its aqueduct, and climb the hills that lead to the Temple of the Sun, the Temple of the Foliated Cross, and the Temple of the Cross (in that sequence).

After your lunch, return to the Palace before climbing the Temple of the Inscriptions, and, finally, visiting the Crypt.

This all assumes that you have allowed yourself only one day in Palenque; and it is perfectly possible to cover the ground in the fashion described. However, a more leisurely two-day stay is advised. You will simply feel cheated if you have so scheduled your time that you can see each place only once. You will want to find time, for example, to study the detail of the magnificent altar of the Temple of the Sun; to understand the significance of the symbols carved upon it—and simply to stand back and absorb its beauty.

You have come a long way—and a fascinating one—to Palenque. Do not fail to absorb and appreciate its many aspects.

THE BUILDINGS OF PALENQUE

PALACE   As the map barely indicates, the Palace is a complex of structures, set on a high mound, and providing a superb view out over the treetops to the north.

Approaching from its western side, you will climb a path to the façade, part of which has collapsed. It is in this southwest area, near the base of the tower, that the latrines are located. The latrines are . . . well, they are just that.

The pillars of this area—and elsewhere, so you must keep your eyes open—have been embellished with lovely stucco bas-reliefs of priests in plumed headdresses receiving offerings, standing on masks representing the earth. Many are badly disfigured by time, but you will still feel their power and beauty. There are many stucco glyphs surrounding these figures that are exceptional for the delicacy of their work. Behind these decorated columns, the rear wall is broken by apertures representing the T-shaped symbol of the wind.

Crossing the open courtyard of the tower, passing between more sculpture-bedecked columns, there is a corbel-vaulted passage whose back wall carries many superb stucco medallions. As you know, it was at Palenque that the handling of the medium of stucco reached its greatest mastery; and you will find this to be true not only of major works, such as columns or medallions, but of individual glyphs as well. Thus, even the smallest detail proves to be worthy of your close attention, and you will want to return to view some of them again.

Access to the tower is achieved across a piece of sloping, broken wall, and is pretty scary if you have no head for heights. But if you do, just take a deep breath and step across! Actually, you will not miss much by not climbing the tower, for its real interest is its unique four-story structure (although you will be reminded of the shorter one at Dzibilchaltún topping the Temple of the Seven Dolls). The topmost story of the Palace has long since disappeared, and the present one represents the best restoration guess of archaeologists. Look over at the second from the right building of the North Group, and you will see what they copied.

Circle back toward the west court, looking again at the magnificent figures on the outer pillars of the West Building. In the court itself, the hut motif appears as decoration; but the real gem here is in its southwest corner, where there is a niche with heads.

The most impressive court is the east one, which you enter by a stair flanked by magnificent hieroglyphs. The far stair is bounded by two sloping panels, each carved with "colossal figures," which, because of their relatively crude workmanship, Stephens considered to come from an older age. They certainly do not resemble the delicacy of all the other work at Palenque; indeed, the farthest right-hand one is a fertility symbol with an abnormally large penis. The workmanship, though, is by no means as rough as that of the idol at Sayil. The features of all the figures are gross and almost distorted, rather than lifelike.

Moving to the south through the far building, you will be at once struck by the Moorish appearance of the trilobate openings that have been cut in the sides of the usual corbeled arch. There is, of course, no such Moorish influence; the builders merely used their device here to lighten the arch itself.

Come west again through the central court to give yourself another opportunity to see the magnificent medallions that line the passage, and prepare to enter the *subterráneos*.

These rooms are beneath the southern buildings of the Palace and probably were used as cells for the priests, but, damp and dank, they are certainly not where you would enjoy living. They may be entered from the tower court, and you will leave them at the south ground level.

Stop before you descend! Light a match and look at the outer face of the arch before you enter the passage. It is of beautifully decorated stucco. And perhaps the loveliest and most touchingly human of all the sculpture of Palenque is centered over the door. Here is a kneeling priestess, her hand curved upward in a supplicating gesture, hidden in the darkness for centuries.

MUSEUM   By now it is about ten o'clock, and the museum is open. In this little building are contained many of the treasures of Palenque, kept on the site rather than abducted to Mexico City. You must not miss this exhibition, for here you can see at close range, in well-lighted surroundings, many items that would otherwise be defaced or decaying. More than anywhere else in the land of the Maya (except for perishable frescoes) the delicate detail of the stucco work of Palenque must be protected if it is to survive.

At the door is a stele, representing a priest standing on a hieroglyph. It was originally found at the foot of the stairway leading to the Temple of the Cross.

While each one of the objects in the museum deserves your attention—it really is a remarkable collection—certain ones should definitely not be overlooked in the midst of so much of interest. Each item in the museum is numbered for your easy identification, and this system (generally moving counterclockwise around the room) is, as far as possible, followed here, although rearrangements may well have been made.

ITEM #2, to the right, is the Slab of 96 Hieroglyphs, which was found at the foot of the tower. Its date (A.D. 783) is interesting because the number 13 recurs in it, a number that the Maya, like ourselves, regarded as particularly significant. The day pictured is 13 Ahau; the month, 13 Muan; at the end of Tun 13.

ITEMS #12 and #16 are modeled clay cylinders from the Temple of the Foliated Cross. They resemble totem poles—mask is stacked on mask. Shown are a bird, the long-nosed Rain God, the God of the Sun, and the God of the Earth.

ITEM #14 is the well-known Panel of the Slaves,

found in an area known as Group IV, buildings located
to the right of the entrance. Beneath a band of hieroglyphs, the central, large figure of a priest is shown,
seated cross-legged on a pillow that rests on the back of
two crouching, mustachioed slaves. On the right the
smaller figure of a priestess rests on a deer; on the left, a
priest holding the Plant of Life (remember the device
on the tail of the serpent entwined on the frieze of the
West Building of the Nunnery at Uxmal?) is seated on a
mask of the Sun God.

ITEMS #19 and #20 are, respectively, the Slab of the
Scribe and that of the Orator. Both were found at the
foot of the tower, and the scenes portrayed are described
by their names.

Now look at this wall and the one directly facing it to
see two magnificent masks of stucco. The simpler of the
two, on the far wall, is believed to be an actual death
mask, cast from the features of a dead priest. The other,
the amazingly beautiful Cara de Palenque, brings to
mind Shelley's "Ozymandias."

. . . a shattered visage lies, whose frown,
And wrinkled lip, and sneer of cold command,
Tell that its sculptor well those passions read
Which yet survive, stamped on these lifeless things,
. . . .
"My name is Ozymandias, king of kings:
Look on my works, ye Mighty, and despair!"
Nothing beside remains. Round the decay

Of that colossal wreck, boundless and bare
The lone and level sands stretch far away.

The jungle of Palenque is far from the land of Arabia
Deserta, but here, too, master artists labored to produce
things of beauty for a civilization that was destined to
pass away.

ITEM #26, a collection of stucco hieroglyphs, are exquisite in their detail. It seems impossible that these
finely executed glyphs, a thousand years old, could have
survived to our time in such beautiful condition.

ITEM #27 is the Panel of the Palace, and was found
still in place in the North Building. At the top center of
a mass of glyphs, a high priest receives offerings from a
priest of the Sun God and a priestess of the Rain Goddess. It is possible that the central figure, rather than
that of a priest, is the young Maize God, Yum Kaax.
The Initial Series (the seven large glyphs at the left
margin) represent one of the few cases where the Mayas
made use of complete human figures to designate num-
bers and chronological periods instead of the conventional bars and dots.

TEMPLE OF THE INSCRIPTIONS AND FUNERARY CRYPT
The exterior stairs of the Temple of the Inscriptions
are easy to climb: it is neither especially high nor steep.
And it is terraced, so there is no awesome drop as you
start down.

After ascending the temple, you find yourself on a

broad platform that affords a magnificent view. On the back walls, giving the temple its name, are huge panels of hieroglyphs, conveying a series of dates stretching over some two hundred years. The outer pillars, framing the five entrance doors, are decorated with human figures in stucco. These represent men and women carrying small children—with faces in the form of masks of Chac and one leg elongated in the shape of a serpent! These were once violently colored: the brilliant yellow of ocherous earths; the scarlet made from the cochineal insect; and the purple from a snail of the coast.

The interior, reached through a slab at the altar of the temple, consists of a steep, corbeled stairway that leads, with one landing, to the Funerary Crypt, which is actually located five feet below ground level. The passage and crypt were discovered in 1952 by Alberto Ruz Lhuillier, who noticed finger holes on the slab and, on lifting it, opened up the rubble-filled stairway. At the landing a ventilation shaft reaches horizontally to the outside of the temple. Notice that at the left side of the steps, conforming to them, is a square duct. This leads directly from the main altar to the sarcophagus itself, like the "psycho-duct" of the Temple of the Seven Dolls at Dzibilchaltún, intended to permit communication between the priests and the dead.

Until the discovery of this crypt, it had been generally accepted that Maya pyramids were simply the substructures for religious buildings or series of temples (in contrast to the Egyptian custom of erecting a pyramid as a mausoleum or tomb for a king). Now, Ruz Lhuillier's excavation changed all that: for here was a magnificent, temple-topped pyramid apparently deliberately designed to cover a crypt, holding the sarcophagus of some great noble or priest. The issue is still not settled, however.

The tomb is below the plaza surrounding the pyramid. Was the tomb built and the mound constructed over it, with the interior access stairway following the stages of construction upward? Or was the pyramid-temple built, and then, following the death of the great man, was it decided to construct a tomb within the mound, and so the stair cut and the tomb set into the solid earth below rather than in the rubble?

In the former case, there is a genuine parallel with the Egyptian mausoleum-pyramid. In the latter, the Mayan temple-pyramid tradition is unbroken; and the later inclusion of a tomb within the structure represents only an alteration of the original design.

The Funerary Crypt, regardless of its origin, is a magnificent sepulcher. There is a high, corbeled ceiling, with additional support given by transverse stone members (like those you will have noticed in the passage on the way down). During the excavation, in the area just in front of the crypt, the skeletons of six young men were found, the "volunteer" guardians of the great man on his journey into the spirit world. Painted on the walls of the crypt, now barely discernible, were stucco reliefs of nine richly dressed personages, the Bolon-ti-Ku, the Lords of Night and of the Nether Worlds. The monolithic sarcophagus is huge, 10 feet long and 7 wide. Seal-

Palenque: Slab from Funerary Crypt, Temple of the Inscriptions

ing it, and now lifted from it, is a superbly decorated
slab (see illustration).

The poor lighting of the crypt makes it most difficult
for you to discern the details, and you will do well to
familiarize yourself with it in advance, so that you will
know what you are looking at.

The central figure on the slab is that of a reclining
man, with bent knees and upraised torso. He rests on a
fearsome mask that represents the God of Earth, with
much of the appearance of a full-face of Chac. Immediately behind him rises a cruciform motif, highly decorated; the transverse arms end in serpents with raised
tails and open jaws, from each of which protrudes a head.
Perched on the top of the cross is a quetzal bird. Masks
of the sun and the moon are beneath the quetzal's head
and tail. Surrounding the whole is a band of glyphs that
bears symbols of various heavenly bodies. On the sides of
the slab are additional date glyphs, setting the year of
the event as A.D. 633.

In the sarcophagus itself was found the skeleton of a
tall man between forty and fifty years of age. He was covered with jade ornaments, with a ring on each finger. A
magnificent mosaic jade mask was also in the sarcophagus. Beneath it were two remarkably fine stucco heads
(the Cara de Palenque is one) that had originally been
part of a temple decoration.

TEMPLE OF THE SUN   As you cross the brook that is
the Río Otulum, look to your left. You will see that it
forks; part of it pours into an underground, vaulted

aqueduct that was used during heavy rains, to drain away the swollen water from the foundations of the Palace.

Ahead of you are three mounded hills, each with a temple carrying a high roof comb. These are, from the left, the Temple of the Cross, the Temple of the Foliated Cross, and the Temple of the Sun. Each of these buildings, and the Temple of the Inscriptions as well, conforms to the same general design: an outer room or portico with heavy supporting pillars and an inner shrine flanked by two small cells. The whole building, with its mansard-type roof, is crowned with a high roof comb, once decorated with stucco figures, now a delicate tracery of holes.

The Temple of the Sun takes its name from the magnificently carved stone shrine, representing two priests worshiping the sun. The sun itself is a rayed, rounded mask looking smilingly down on a platform representing earth, which is supported by two crouching slaves. The sun is centered on two crossed spears whose hilts are turned upward, which may connote a connection with Chac. The priests, one portrayed as larger than the other to indicate his superiority, stand on two kneeling figures. The whole is framed by a wide band of glyphs, in this case dating A.D. 642.

TEMPLE OF THE FOLIATED CROSS   The cross must not be confused with the Christian cross. Rather, it is a representation of the Tree of Life, and, in this case, its branching arms terminate in flowing leaves. Its vertical bar, supported by the earth, ends in a human head, from whose neck hangs a medallion of the Sun God. On this head is perched a quetzal, looking at a tiny deer held as an offering by the taller of the two priests. (At the Temple of the Sun, the smaller of the two priests held the bird offering.) The surrounding glyphs here give the date as A.D. 692. It was in this temple, you will recall, that the totem poles you saw in the museum were found.

TEMPLE OF THE CROSS   The panel that lends its name to this temple has been moved to Mexico City, but it is still well worth the short climb to see the carved slabs that flank the doorway. They have had an interesting history, too, for at one time they were taken from their natural place and set into the pillars of the Church of Santo Domingo, in the plaza alongside the Hotel Palenque. Here Stephens saw them, and wanted desperately to procure them. But he was not a Mexican citizen, so he could not do so. He found that the rightful owners were two maiden ladies of Palenque; and he very seriusly considered marrying one of them in order to secure title! Fortunately, a bout of fever struck him and he was compelled to leave before achieving his aim.

The left-hand jamb shows a young man, but it is now quite cracked. The right one is, however, virtually intact, and is a magnificent portrayal of a toothless old man with an elaborate headdress, draped in a jaguar skin. He is smoking! Incidentally, he probably represents not a priest but Itzamná, the son of the principal god, and the senior member of the Maya divinity. For some reason, God the Father, the Creator, is seldom mentioned; His Son, portrayed as an old man with toothless jaws and sunken cheeks, stands at the head of the Maya pantheon.

GETTING TO PALENQUE—AND WHAT TO DO THERE

It is not difficult to get to Palenque. The principal problem is that no one seems particularly interested in helping you do so.

The best way to go—and it will still be the most interesting, even should direct air connections become available—is to fly on Mexicana from Mérida to Villahermosa (the plane touches down in Campeche and Ciudad del Carmen, places you may well wish to visit).

Stay overnight at the HOTEL MANSUR in Villahermosa. For in the Parque La Venta (near the airport) is one of the most extraordinary collections of archaeological objects ever assembled.

A relatively few miles distant from Villahermosa, infinitely separated in time, was the ancient Olmec city of La Venta. The Olmec culture is believed to be the mother lode of all other Mexican civilizations: the Aztec, the Huastec, the Zapotec-Mixtec . . . and the Maya. The original La Venta was located in a great swamp, utterly cut off from the outside world, yet it contained monolithic images that weighed up to thirty tons, with the nearest quarries hundreds of miles away. The archaeologists have transported La Venta's monuments and set them up in a jungle setting in the Parque La Venta. A visit to them is fantastic! You will never forget coming down a trail and there, as you round a clump of bamboo, you are confronted with a giant head, glowering fiercely from a green mound.

In the evening, you'll have time to stroll leisurely around this simple town, and enjoy a glimpse of a more natural side of Mexican life. The food in the Hotel Mansur is very good (the *flan* especially so). In the morning, before your early lunch, you'll have plenty of time to visit a pleasant museum in the town.

You will have to make arrangements for a taxi, or hired car, to take you to Teapa, some thirty miles south over potholed roads that do not permit speedy travel, to catch one of the thrice-weekly trains to Palenque. This should cost you around 100 pesos, plus a tip to the helpful driver.

The train has a Pullman car and a diner, but you'll have more fun in a first-class carriage. (Don't attempt second- or third-class, they're not for you.) The trip to Palenque takes three and a half hours, depending. . . . Actually, you will arrive pretty much on time, since the schedule is so flexible that the train, a Diesel-engined one, just moseys along the way.

The occasion of the arrival of the train in Teapa is practically a fiesta. Women set up booths along the side of the track to sell foodstuffs and necessities; a sweetbread seller arrives, his six-by-three-foot tray balanced on a rope "halo" on his head. Soldiers in a multiplicity of uniforms slouch around. The whole town, not just the traveling public, seems to have gathered. And if you have a Polaroid camera, everybody will push to get into your picture—so that they can see themselves in sixty seconds in color!

The fare is negligible, but you will still have your first-class coach (one whose cleanliness and general state of repair would be a credit to some of our commuter trains!) pretty much to yourselves. Little girls, carrying pots of *tortillas, enchiladas,* or rice, act as the dining facilities for the public, but you would be wise to pass them up.

Finally, after all have fed and rested, the train gets on its leisurely way. And you will want to walk back to the diner, not only for some *chocolate hecho con agua,* but for the sheer fascination of seeing how the Mexicans live.

The second- and third-class coaches are packed with people of all sorts, happy people, singing and talking incessantly together. There will be cowboys in colorful *serapes,* dark-skinned priests and nuns, *campesinos* from all localities—and all will be smiling. Sweet-faced women in *huipiles* will be modestly, but unconcernedly, nursing babies; and children will be scrambling everywhere. Maya men in broad straw hats, white shirts, and white cut-off trousers will be carrying their ever-present *machetes,* woven henequen carry-all bags, and calabash water gourds. Don't stare. Don't take pictures. Just walk slowly, smile peacefully, and absorb it all.

Don't read a book on the train. Look out the window and see the countryside change. From the low coastal plain of Tabasco, you are rising into the highlands of Chiapas. (You are now in the state of Chiapas and have come quite a way from Yucatán!)

Palms and rubber plantations give way to cattle spreads. Swamps dry up and misty mountains rise. Small huts beside the track have little children in front of them, waving, as the train goes by.

There's a brook running swiftly, making a miniature waterfall into the ditch that follows the right of way. There are countless banana trees, with broad green leaves; and bird-of-paradise plants, with their orange, red, and yellow spikes, are a common sight.

Every so often the train stops at what you know must be a station, for you saw the list, with its numbered kilometer designations, on the big board when you bought your ticket at Teapa. The train labors slowly upward, and you watch the white markers as they tell you that you are getting closer to Palenque.

Arriving at the depot of Palenque, which is about five miles out of town away from the ruins, you will find that there are plenty of taxis available to take you to the Hotel Palenque. About 10 pesos, plus a tip for helping with the luggage, is correct.

The accommodations at the HOTEL PALENQUE are roughly comparable to those of a small motel in the States. They are clean, with private toilet and shower. A small, rather primitive restaurant is open. The food is not good, but you can certainly get a meal. Eggs are suggested, or a thin, rather tough steak. Bottled water here, definitely. Or, better yet, get them to squeeze you as much grapefruit juice as you can. (If they run out of fruit, they'll send a boy for more.) It is, by the way, *jugo de pómelo*, not *jugo de torjona* that you should ask for and get. The *pómelo* is a non-acid type of grapefruit that is simply delicious.

Don't expect too much of the Hotel Palenque. It is clean, the people couldn't be nicer or more helpful, but their facilities are limited—as is their experience with the American tourist. You may even encounter language difficulty here, but with smiles and a mutual attempt at understanding, you'll be able to fulfill your simple needs and enjoy yourself. The number of rooms is limited, so when you make your arrangements in advance, be sure to specify that you want twins, with bath, in the new section.

There is a restaurant near (a quarter of a mile downhill . . . that means uphill afterward) the ruins, HERTA's. Do *not* attempt to go here at night. Insist to your travel agent that you will dine at the Hotel Palenque (and breakfast, too). The reason is that the restaurant is located down an unlit path through the jungle that may be teeming with any sort of reptile. In place of the usual catsup bottle on the dining table, you'll be shocked to see a bottle of snake-bite serum.

Lunch at Herta's is supposed to be good; but this depends on how Herta happens to feel that day. The facilities are filthy . . . unbelievably so. But it's near the ruins, so convenient that "everybody" goes there. For

your second day's lunch at Palenque, why not try ordering at the hotel, *the night before,* a couple of egg sand-
wiches and a bottle of grapefruit juice?

You will do well, in fact, to order in advance at the
hotel. They are not geared for fast service, nor do they
adapt readily; but they will make every effort to fulfill
your desires. Thus, before you go to bed, tell them at
what exact time you want your breakfast (and allow for
the fact that it won't be ready then); and exactly what
you want to eat. At the same time, but as a separate operation, tell them when you want your sandwich-and-
grapefruit-juice lunch. Be sure that everything is clear,
for they try so hard, and want so desperately to be helpful, that what you want to express in Spanish and what
they understand do not necessarily coincide.

One reason why you may decide to spend two full days
at Palenque, to absorb and appreciate its beauty, is a
matter of necessity. The train on which you came from
Teapa to Palenque continues on to Mérida; but it only
runs three days a week. (On alternate days it runs in the
reverse direction, passing through Palenque at an un-
earthly hour of the night; the train rests on Sunday.)
There is a freight train without adequate accommodations that travels daily, but it is not recommended for
passengers.

The best plan is to take the train from Palenque back
to Mérida, this time riding in your comfortable Pullman
and eating in the dining car. As always, the train takes its
time, but you'll get into Mérida around lunchtime, and
be able to see some more of the countryside en route.

There are alternatives to this method of transportation; but the one outlined here is easy and pleasant. For example, in Villahermosa, it is quite practical to charter a plane from a Señor de la Torre and be in Palenque in half an hour, and out the same day. Or go up in the train and rent a taxi in Palenque for the drive back to Villahermosa. This will cost you about 350 to 500 pesos, and will take about five hours over some rough roads, but you'll see a new and different land.

In any event, train, plane, or car, don't miss Palenque.

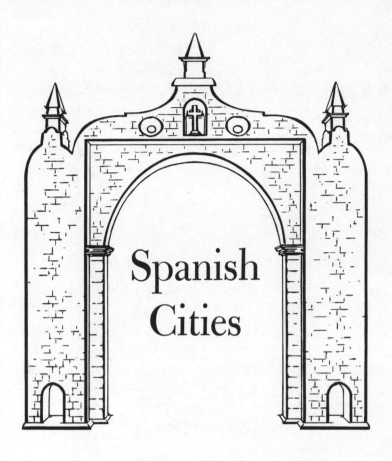

Spanish
Cities

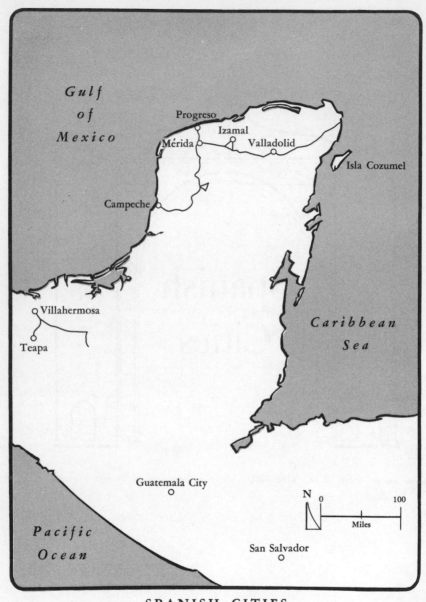

SPANISH CITIES

Mérida

Don't treat Mérida just as a convenient, pleasant stopping place on your way somewhere else. The city is very old, founded in 1542 by Francisco de Montejo, the *adelantado,* or governor, of Yucatán.

There are two means of transportation to use in Mérida: your feet, and a *calesa.* Both must be used to appreciate the city fully. There is no substitute for strolling in the park; not even the leisurely clop-clop of a horse's hooves takes its place.

Start with a *calesa* ride to orient yourself. These carriages are beautifully painted and clean, but the horse and its driver are growing old. You will quite probably find that your driver does not speak English, but enlist the aid of a passerby to give him directions. The rate should be about 10 pesos for an hour's drive, plus a tip for his help as a "guide"—for, if you do speak Spanish, he can tell you a lot. Most *calesas* are found in a row along the PARQUE CEPADA, a very delightful little park.

Before you start your ride, look at the IGLESIA DE LA

TERCERA ORDEN across the street. It is quite lovely but not especially noteworthy inside. But notice the lattice effect sculptured on its exterior. As you found at Uxmal, this is an ancient religious symbol, stemming from the woven mats that were used in temple construction before the time of stone buildings.

As a suggested route, tell your driver to go first to the CHURCH OF THE MEJORADA, which faces on a dry little park a few blocks from the Hotel Panamericana. You will get a nice view of an old and somewhat disintegrating Spanish church with its heavy wood doors, but there is nothing here to make you wish to dismount.

You are, though, at the edge of the old city, marked by a MOORISH ARCH, one of three that still survive from part of the original city wall. Turn right here, in the direction of the CHURCH OF SAN CRISTOBAL.

Keep a sharp lookout on the northeast walls of the street corners to your right. After three blocks or so, you will see that one is marked by two plaques set into the wall of the building. Tell your driver to stop. He and the horse will be happy to do so. The lower plaque carries an inscription in Latin, dedicating the area, and bearing the date 1627. The upper stone is unique, and nobody seems to know anything about it or pay any attention to it, and certainly your driver will not know how to find it unless you tell him. It is one of the old, old street signs from the days when an illiterate populace recognized only that they were at the "Street of the Old Woman," or that of the "Flamingo." (Some of these are in the Mérida museum.) But this one shows an Angel (perhaps Gabriel?) with a trumpet in one hand and a palm branch in the other. Cut into the stone is the name of the street: "Calle de Ymposible y Cebencio." Fascinating!

Even if you are a scholar, and one thoroughly versed in Spanish at that, you may not be able to comprehend the meaning of this phrase. Actually, it is something like the motto of the Seabees: "The difficult we do immediately, the impossible takes a little time." How is this idea derived from "Ymposible y Cebencio"? Well, the old Spaniards didn't spell very well (not much better than Chaucer did in English, as a matter of fact), and tended to write down words as they sounded. "Ymposible" is easy . . . *Imposible* . . . or, in English, Impossible. As for the rest of it, substitute an *s* for the *c*, and a *v* for the *b*, split it into two words, and "Cebencio" becomes "se vencio." Freely translated, the sign now reads: "The Street That Was Impossible But Was Conquered." (And, judging from the pot-holed condition of Mérida's streets today, not too bad a description!)

The CHURCH OF SAN CRISTOBAL, nearby, is a huge edifice, but, like so many Spanish churches, without anything particular to recommend it. Again, just seeing its exterior is sufficient.

Drive past the Market (Mercado), just to fix its location in your mind. Resist the temptation to go in now, for you will walk there later, and you should get on with your *calesa* tour. Note that there is a little park opposite it, where there is a *calesa* stand, should you later need help in carrying home your purchases.

From here swing out to the ARCH OF SAN JUAN—
not that it is particularly different from the two you
have already seen, but you will get a look at more of
the city on the way.

From here it is only a few blocks to the CHURCH OF
SAN JUAN BAUTISTA, located on a pretty park with a "su-
permercado" across the way. Again, nothing special to
see here; for you are storing up your church visiting for
the magnificent Cathedral.

Next, circle the PLAZA MAYOR, the beautiful, tree-
shaded square that is the center of the city's life; the
huge park measures six hundred feet per side. Along the
north front is the green arcaded GOVERNMENT PALACE;
to the west, behind white arcades, is what was formerly
the home of Doña Peon, where Stephens stayed when
he visited Mérida; now it is the HOUSE OF THE MUNICI-
PALITY. On the east side is the great Cathedral, and on
the south, the Montejo house, both of which you will
want to investigate much more thoroughly.

Dismiss your *calesa* here, for it is only a short distance
to your hotel, and stroll around awhile, getting the feel
of this heart of the city.

The MONTEJO HOUSE, as a private home, is opened to
the public during certain hours of the day, not as a
money-making venture, but as a courtesy to the interested visitor. The house, as has been mentioned, was
built in 1549. Francisco Montejo the younger had no
male heir, and the home was inherited by a great-
granddaughter, who had married Don Simon Peon.

Before you enter, the outside is well worth a careful

inspection, for it is one of the finest examples of Mexican plateresque extant. This type of decoration is reminiscent of the work of Spanish silversmiths (*plateros*), and consists of delicately carved stucco, which was popular in the Spanish renaissance in the early sixteenth century.

Despite the theme, which glorifies the first Montejo, the work was done by Mayas; and it is interesting to consider that these remote descendants of the builders of Palenque lost none of their skill in the medium. Narrow windows to the right of the entrance frame on their entablatures the coats of arms of successive generations of the Montejos. But the real interest in them lies in the Grecian-type caryatids that sustain the lintels, for their bodies are that distinctively Mayan device—entwined serpents.

Over the heavily decorated doorway two armored knights are on guard, standing on two crouching Indians (recalling the stance of the Maya priests in Palenque's Temple of the Sun). Smaller and lower than the knightly figures are two extraordinary beings carrying clubs— dressed in feathers, they conjure a remote memory of the times of Kukulcán.

Inside, the house is arranged around a tree-filled patio, whose greenery was brought back from Asia, Africa, and Europe in the ships of the family traders. On three sides of the patio is a broad veranda, opening into various family rooms. The northwest room is the formal living room, with fine antique furniture and a series of family portraits, including one of Don Simon Peon, Ste-

phens' host and friend. It was Don Simon who showed
Stephens the original grant of Uxmal from the Spanish
crown in 1673. The fascinating traditional "deed of liv-
ery of seisin" sets forth that "In the place called the edifices of Uxmal and its lands, I took by the hand the said
Lorenzo de Evia [a Peon ancestor], and he walked with
me all over Uxmal and its buildings, opened and shut
some doors, cut within the space some trees, picked up
fallen stones and threw them down, drew water from
one of the aguadas of the said place of Uxmal, and performed other acts of possession."

In the far corner on a table are some Mayan pottery
and clay figurines, which were bought from the Indians.
The present owner explains their "genuineness" by noting that the country Maya are growing pretty sophisticated. When they learn that a road is to be built that
would cut through an ancient mound, they hurry there
and do some amateur excavating—or is it "salting" the
mine?—offering for sale the pieces that they have thus
"found" there!

You will also be interested in the fine carrara marble
floors, whose blocks came back as ballast in ships that
had once carried logwood (for dye) to Italy. The
comedor, or dining room, has an exceptionally lovely
old chandelier, and its walls are covered with damask.
The walls of the building, by the way, are 3 feet thick,
made of stone blocks with earth fill between—for defensive purposes.

Before you enter the CATHEDRAL, pause. This is a

House of God; approach it reverently. The crowds that
flow in and out of it like inexorable tides are worshipers;
do not disturb their prayers and meditations.

Such prayer and meditation are part of the atmosphere of a church, and can greatly add to your appreciation of its art. By participating with the crowd in
their worship you enhance your feeling for the people
around you, and thus gain an added understanding of
the object that you are seeing. Find the altar, picture,
or statue in which you are interested—and then make
yourself as inconspicuous as possible. (In a land of small,
dark people this may prove difficult for a six-foot American and his fair wife!) Absorb the mood, and discover
how much more you will see and feel.

You will not want to miss seeing the lovely and interesting Altar of Santo Cristo de los Ampollas (Christ of
the Blisters). This is the first altar to the left of the main
altar. In addition to being a fine piece of sculpture, this
life-sized crucifix has a fascinating history. About A.D.
1600 the Mayas in the town of Ichmul reported to their
priest that a tree near his church burned each night, yet
was never consumed by the fires; each morning it appeared exactly as it did the day before. Confronted with
this miraculous occurrence, the priest ordered that the
tree be cut down and carved into a figure of the cruci-
fied Christ. This was done, and the statue graced the
altar of that little church until 1643. In that year, the
church containing it was destroyed by fire. But in its
ashes was found the carved crucifix, whole and un-

harmed, save that the body of Christ was covered by blisters! Moved to the Mérida Cathedral, the crucifix has become an object of great reverence.

On the south wall, over the easternmost door, hangs a huge panoramic painting showing the Mayan king Tutul Xiu's formal call on the Adelantado Montejo. In its background is shown a view of the Mayan capital of T'ho, in all its barbaric splendor. This visit occurred only seventeen days after the founding of Mérida on that site in 1542, and was of vital importance to the Spaniards, for Tutul Xiu came not as a warrior but as an admirer of the bravery of the white men, and desired to see their religious ceremonies. Montejo ordered a chaplain of the army, also shown in the painting, to celebrate "a solemn Adoration of the Holy Cross" and Tutul Xiu became a convert to Christianity. He stayed in the Spaniards' camp for two months, was instructed, and was baptized Melchor. As a Christian, Melchor urged his fellow lords of the western area to submit to the Spaniards, and thus further fighting was kept to a minimum.

Be sure to see the patio of the Hotel Panamericana, for this was once part of a Victorian mansion, and is beautifully decorated with fine plaster work in full relief, picturing fluttering doves against dark colors.

Artistry in the use of ornamental stucco seems to be a part of Maya culture, a beauty of form that reached its height in Palenque a thousand years ago. Yet the work in this patio is worthy of this tradition; and it is fully comparable with that produced by the Italian artists who, working under the direction of Robert West, decorated the proud houses on St. Stephen's Green in Dublin.

Indeed, there is a real similarity between the two, both in subject and in handling. In both cases the doves seem almost to fly from the walls, so delicate and rounded are they. Interestingly, in Ireland they were made less striking by setting them against a pastel blue or pink background; while here in Mérida the strong contrast between the white doves and the reddish-purple of the cornice is vivid and impressive.

The MARKET covers an area of several blocks east and south of the Plaza Mayor. Much of it is in a huge, barn-like building; the floor space is split into hundreds of tiny stalls, each occupied by an individual entrepreneur. Certain portions are given over to foodstuffs, while others are devoted to clothing, hardware, or household necessities.

In all honesty, you'll probably get most of your fun from window-shopping here. Although you will find that there are certain tourist items available, this is fundamentally a genuine marketplace serving the needs of a city. However, should you want to bring a native hammock home for your porch, you will find a large selection available. Those made of henequen are more "native," but they do tend to be a bit prickly, and the nylon ones, also locally made, are better. String bags for carrying your purchases, some decorated with colorful scenes of pyramids, donkeys, or masks, are durable and inexpensive.

You may encounter problems in the clothing section.

Most of the shops in the market cater to the lower-income groups, and carry products of an inferior quality. Certainly, if you are a good bargainer and can recognize the real value of materials, you will do well here; but as a general rule, you will do better to purchase clothing in more conventional stores. Sizes will be a bother if your purchases are intended as gifts, for the Mayas are not built as we are, but are shorter and stockier. So measure everything you look at and be certain of the fit.

Huipiles, of course, are intended to be blocky and shapeless, essentially a rectangular bag of white cotton with a circular neck, decorated with bands of colorful embroidery. If you are thinking of purchasing one (or a blouse of this pattern), do a lot of comparison shopping first. Do not be misled into buying the cheaper machine-embroidered models when you can purchase better quality materials decorated with cross-stitched handwork. Generally, you'll find better bargains in the interior of the marketplace, while the stores exhibiting on the perimeter cater more to the tourist trade.

For men, the *guayabera* is the item to be sought. These loose-fitting white shirt-jackets are cool, comfortable, and attractive. Again, size and quality is a basic problem; and if you're like most men you'll take the easy way and do your buying at a more conventional store. (Camiseria Canul, on Calle 59, near the Hotel Panamericana, has good values and selections.)

There are several liquor stores just outside the main market, if you want to be assured of reasonable prices for that bottle you are allowed to bring back duty-free.

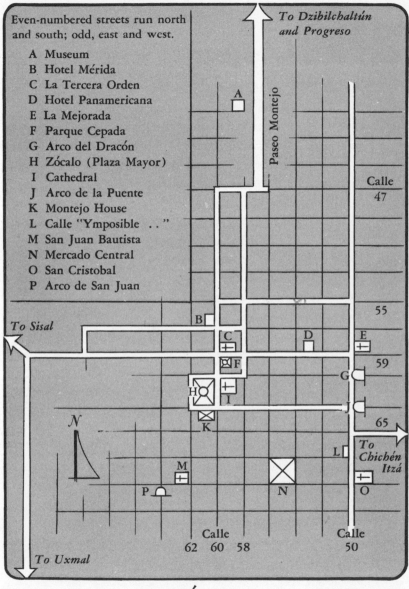

Even-numbered streets run north
and south; odd, east and west.

A Museum
B Hotel Mérida
C La Tercera Orden
D Hotel Panamericana
E La Mejorada
F Parque Cepada
G Arco del Dracón
H Zócalo (Plaza Mayor)
I Cathedral
J Arco de la Puente
K Montejo House
L Calle "Ymposible .."
M San Juan Bautista
N Mercado Central
O San Cristobal
P Arco de San Juan

*To Dzibilchaltún
and Progreso*

Paseo Montejo

Calle
47

To Sisal

55

59

65

*To
Chichén
Itzá*

Calle
62 60 58

Calle
50

To Uxmal

MÉRIDA

Bazaar del arte

Just because you won't be doing any purchasing is no excuse to not visit the colorful food-selling areas of the market. If you are squeamish, stay away from the meat and fish sections, for sanitary conditions are not as you find them in the States. But don't miss the displays of vegetables, for here is a good occasion to use your color film. In one part, for instance, Mayan women, each wearing *huipil* and *rebozo,* sit cross-legged on the ground languidly fanning flies from their stocks of ground *chile, frijoles,* or lima beans, which glisten in brilliant reds, blacks, and whites. In others, squash, tomatoes, and oranges are piled in profusion, providing a lovely spectacle.

It is not a market to compare in interest to the tourist with that of Chichicastenango, or even of urban Guatemala, but you will find it interesting nonetheless.

Izamal

This Spanish city contains much that is Mayan as well. Located on a side road between Mérida and Chichén Itzá, it represents only a short detour from your main route, and well repays the slight effort involved.

While Izamal may be reached on your way to Chichén by taking the left-hand fork after the town of Hoctun, about thirty miles from Mérida, it is suggested that you visit it on your return trip instead, if only to take advantage of rounding out a full American-plan day at the hotel.

On your way back to Mérida, then, you will find a sign in the small village of Libre Union, where you will make a sharp right. In any case, you will pass through charming Maya villages, with houses of thatched roofs and white-washed walls.

Too, it is true that your approach to Izamal from the direction of Chichén Itzá is highly spectacular. In this way, as you emerge from a small village into broad fields of henequen, you see in the middle distance the bell towers of the pale yellow adobe Cathedral; and, to its right, equally high and as massively imposing, the dark bulk of an ancient pyramid, now overgrown and desolate. Stephens describes it as "a stupendous mound," while *Terry's Guide to Mexico* says that it "evokes a strange, brooding atmosphere that is unique." In any event, by approaching Izamal from the south and east, rather than from the direction of Mérida, you get the greatest impact of the contrast between these two relics of the Spanish and the Mayan cultures.

There is nothing special to be gained by climbing the PYRAMID except for an expansive view, although someone has erected a rude wooden cross on its top. But it is most worth your while to ascend into the CATHEDRAL. You actually do ascend, for it was built in 1553 by the famous Bishop Landa upon the Mayan Castle of the Kings, a pyramid that he had torn down, and which provided the basic stones for his edifice. In fact, if you will look into a patio on the left as you enter, you will see a richly carved Chac nose resting under a banana tree!

The nave of the Cathedral has some rather fine Gothic ribbed vaulting, but is otherwise uninspiring. But note that the central piece over the high altar is of peculiarly plain wood, painted blue with a gold star at its center.

Now climb to the *camarin*, a small chapel used not for services, but for reflection and meditation. Here the altar is backed by a statue of the Virgin and Child, resplendent in silver, almost out of place in this austere room.

But in fact there is a direct relationship between these

apparent discrepancies. For, during services in the Cathedral, the statue is pivoted around, the doors over the central main altar are opened, and the Virgin and Child from the *camarin* appear as a part of the principal church!

On the wall of the *camarin* is a contemporary portrait of Bishop Landa, the extraordinary man who both destroyed all relics of Maya culture by his book-burning and preserved its calendrics by ordering them translated into Spanish. Indeed, it is upon his *Relación de las Cosas de Yucatán* that much of our knowledge of Mayan life and customs is based.

On certain feast days in the fall of the year, a statue of a black Christ is brought into the Cathedral from its place in a nearby village church. This church is a mission, and is kept locked except when services are being held, so it is difficult to arrange to see the statue. Very ancient and carved from dark wood, it is especially revered by the natives—as are similar statues in other Latin countries—because, as they say, it is "small and dark, like one of us."

Progreso

Progreso is, of course, not a Spanish city in the strict sense of having links to antiquity, but is merely the seaport of Mérida. But since you have come out on the northern road to visit Dzibilchaltún, and since there is a pleasant place to eat lunch nearby, Los Cocoteros, you really should drive out on the amazing pier.

Due north into the Gulf of Mexico a broad roadway stretches nearly two miles over the tidal flats to terminate in a pier head that can accommodate four or more ocean-going freighters. A railroad spur is also on the roadway so that the transfer of goods aboard can be readily handled.

Here you will see bales of sisal, the pale yellow hemp that grew as the gray-green henequen, being loaded for future manufacture in Europe into bags and burlap. And you will see the silver fifty-gallon drums, stenciled with a pyramid and a bee, that hold one of Yucatán's greatest treasures, the slightly bittersweet dark honey that is prized by the Germans and the Swiss. For this

Yucatecan honey, produced by stingless bees, has become an important export, rising in value as that of
henequen fiber shrinks in competition with the world's
synthetics.

Apiculture also played an important part in the ceremonial life of the ancient Maya. (In case you are not
familiar with that word, on your drive back to Mérida,
look for a factory-like group of buildings on your left—
"La Sociedad de Apicultura de Yucatán, S.A."—which
houses the cooperative where this honey is collected and
barreled.)

The ancient Maya had two principal feasts connected
with bee culture, celebrated by the owners of hives. One
was directed to the flowers, so that there might be an
abundance of blossoms upon which the bees might feast.
The other was intended to influence the bees to produce
more. It was for this latter feast that honey was brewed
into Xtabentun, and, as Sylvanus Morley writes, "heavy
drinking of this beverage concluded the ceremony."

Campeche

This walled city was built by the Spaniards in the late seventeenth century as a protection against the pirates who were then roaming the Caribbean and the Gulf of Mexico. No less than eleven fortifications (*baluartes*) form a tight ring that seals off the central city even today, in spite of breaches made to permit some streets.

These fortifications are massive and solid, built to withstand assault from land and from sea. There are two ancient entrances: the PUERTO DE TIERRA and PUERTO DEL MAR, through whose outlying walls a car must zigzag today.

The individual forts have been put to other purposes, for an excellent archaeological museum now occupies the FORTRESS OF SOLEDAD, to the north of the GATE OF THE SEA. Remember that only about an hour's drive up the main highway to Mérida is the Mayan city of Etzná, with its five-story palace; and not far up the coast is the island of Jaina, famous for its ancient pottery figurines, dating from about A.D. 650.

The FORTRESS OF SAN CARLOS now houses government offices; the museum covering the colonial and pirate periods that once was there has been moved out of town to the south.

But Campeche was old long before the fortifications were built, for here is where Cortés and his *conquistadores* landed in 1517. The city itself was founded officially in 1540, with the laying of the cornerstone of the huge cathedral that dominates the north side of the Plaza Mayor.

The oldest religious site is that of the CHURCH OF SAN FRANCISCO, at the spot where the first Mass was ever said in the New World. Here, too, is the baptistery where the grandson of Cortés was christened, still in use today.

In the town itself, two of the original houses of the TENIENTES DEL REY, the king's lieutenants, still exist, although much has changed from the old days. One, altered beyond recognition, is now the HOTEL COLONIAL. The other, located near 14th and 53rd Streets, is now a warehouse for chicle, and is worth seeing on that account alone! For here the owners—kindly, cheerful people—will be happy to show you this basic component of chewing gum: packed in neat bales for shipment to the States, and also in the original, rough, burlap-wrapped fifty-kilo bundles, exactly as they were brought in from the forests on the backs of Indian gatherers. A well, no longer usable, still occupies the center of the courtyard; and ancient beams of sapote wood ceil the gallery. But look toward the left grillwork as you stand at the massive entrance door. There, still embedded, is a fragment of broken tile, picturing a daintily dressed couple dancing together, the last survivor of a panel that once decorated the gallery where Spanish ladies sat and fanned themselves nearly five hundred years ago.

Another relic of the old times is the so-called PUENTE DE LOS PERROS (Bridge of the Dogs), which is located in the *alameda* section beyond the Gate of the Land. It is named in honor of the Dominican missionaries whose zeal in seeking converts caused them to be called the "Dogs of God."

There is a fascinating building near the Fortress of San Carlos. It has seen many uses, but is now the library of the university. Once it was a church, with a contrasting tiled façade that is reminiscent of the cathedral at Siena in Italy. The left spire, containing a belfry, attests to this use. But the right spire changes your thinking, for it was later made into a lighthouse, complete with lens and high-powered lamp!

And there is also CAMPECHE NUEVO, the new city that is the pride of the citizens. Built outside the old walls, on filled land along the *malecón,* the seawall drive, is a government complex, the high-rise PALACIO DEL PODER and a low, egg-shaped building that houses the Supreme Court. Both are very modern in appearance, quite a contrast to the old town with its pleasant shabbiness that Terry calls "one of the most truly charming places in Mexico."

Notice the two mosaic murals on the Palacio del Poder. Stretching the lengths of the east and west façades, the former depicts the transition of Campeche building from the days of the ancient Maya, through the planning of the fortress (the white-faced, bearded Spaniard hunched over his map is most interesting), to the wonders of the present. The latter mural shows the stages of the economy of the land, from the cultivation of maize to the industrial laborer of today.

And, speaking of the economy, have you eaten the tiny Campeche shrimps yet? They are delicious, sweet, and fresh.

But the real beauty of Campeche is reserved for twilight—*entre dos luces,* as the Spanish poetically call it. From the balcony of your room at the HOTEL BALUARTES, the Gulf of Mexico stretches in a semicircle before you. The sea is calm. The winds have died with the sunset. Color, brilliantly roaring in flame and gold, lights the whole sky. And on the shrimpers anchored just offshore the riding lights begin to go on. The darkness settles, and the white lights look like a city at sea. A hundred or more boats are there, some nested together, some anchored alone, but with their masthead lights bobbing like an animated village street. So we not only have seen Old Campeche, and Campeche Nuevo, but Campeche de las Luces as well.

Index

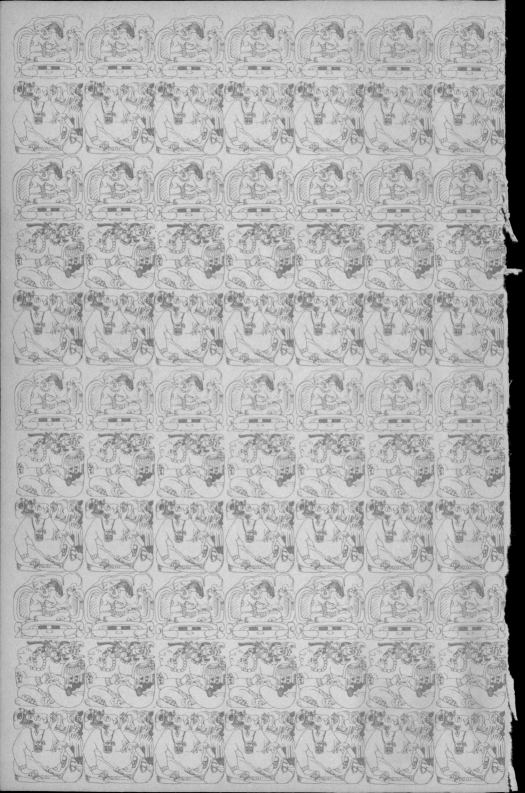